DAILY POETRY

Carol Simpson

 GoodYearBooks

An Imprint of ScottForesman
A Division of HarperCollinsPublishers

Acknowledgments

The author wishes to thank Katie Carpenter and Kristy McGunnigal for sharing their original poetry, which is printed in this book. Thank you to Ryan Oehlert, who wrote the recipe and drew the picture which appear in the section about "Foods I Like." Thank you also to my mother, Ruby Bailey, who spent many hours writing poems that did not get included in this book. Good luck to her in getting her work published elsewhere. Thanks, also, for her help in writing the words of "Cute Pig," which is in this book.

GoodYear Books

are available for most basic curriculum subjects plus many enrichment areas. For more GoodYearBooks, contact your local bookseller or education dealer. For a complete catalog with information about other GoodYearBooks, please write:

GoodYearBooks
Scott Foresman
1900 East Lake Avenue
Glenview, IL 60025

ISBN 0-673-36172-1

456789-EQ-02 01 00 99 98 97

Contents

•••

9.8.98

From *Daily Poetry* published by GoodYearBooks. Copyright © 1995 Carol Simpson.

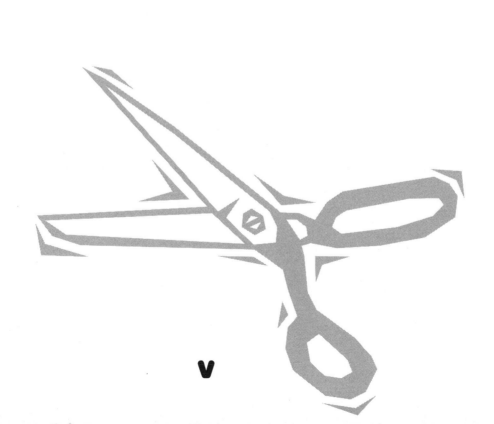

v

Suggested Bibliography

As you read the lists of related poems with each theme, you will notice numbers in parentheses at the ends of the listings. These numbers correspond to the following books which were used when selecting the related poems.

1. *Poetry Place Anthology* (Scholastic, 1990).

2. *Sing a Song of Popcorn* (Scholastic, 1988).

3. *The Random House Book of Poetry for Children* (Random House, 1983).

4. *Side by Side: Poems to Read Together* (Simon & Schuster, 1988).

5. *The Merry-Go-Round Poetry Book* (Delacorte, 1989).

6. *Animals Animals* (Philomel Books, 1989).

7. *A Very First Poetry Book* (Oxford University Press, 1988).

8. *Another Second Poetry Book* (Oxford University Press, 1988).

9. *A Child's Garden of Verses* (Oxford University Press, 1966/1990).

10. *The Usborne Book of Funny Poems* (Usborne, 1990).

11. *Noisy Poems* (Oxford University Press, 1987).

12. *Pass the Poems Please* (Wild Things Press, 1989).

13. *I Never Saw a Purple Cow* (Little, Brown, 1990).

14. *Poems Children Will Sit Still For* (Scholastic, 1969).

15. *More Poetry for Holidays* (Scholastic, 1973).

16. *If I Were in Charge of the World* (Macmillan, 1981).

17. *Butterscotch Dreams* (Heinemann, 1987).

18. *Crackers and Crumbs* (Heinemann, 1990).

19. *If Only I Could Fly* (Juliahouse, 1984).

20. *Let Me Be . . . the Boss* (Boyds Mills, 1992).

21. *Where the Sidewalk Ends* (Harper & Row, 1974).

22. *The New Kid on the Block* (Scholastic, 1984).

From *Daily Poetry* published by GoodYearBooks. Copyright © 1995 Carol Simpson.

HOW TO USE THIS BOOK

For years teachers have shared poetry with their students on Friday afternoons when the work was nearing its end and the workbook pages were done. Poetry-sharing was a quiet, almost contemplative event. It was a time for listening and thinking—not necessarily a time for fun and learning. Today, however, many educators recognize poetry as a valuable tool in teaching children essential language skills. Children enjoy and appreciate poetry, especially the rhyme and rhythm in poetry's verse form. Why not capitalize on that enjoyment and on the children's ability to learn simple poems, and then use that knowledge to teach many important skills?

The purpose of this book is to provide teachers with a variety of poems (enough for one each week) that can be used to teach language and other skills. Ideas for extending each poem with writing, phonics, and other kinds of lessons are suggested and can be adjusted to meet the needs of individual classrooms or students. You will also find lists of trade books and other poems that deal with the basic theme of the selected poem.

Poems are organized under six basic topics: My World, Animals, Mother Nature, Seasons & Holidays, Fantasy, and Colors & Numbers. Listed under each topic are the sub-topics with their suggested poems, trade books, and activities. The poems are organized to be selected as the topic arises, and do not have to be done in sequential order from cover to cover. Most of the extending and writing activities can be adapted to a variety of poems, thus allowing you to be flexible in choosing works to present to your students. Depending upon your grade level and the ability of your students, you may want to select poems and activities that are either easier or more difficult.

A poem can be used to teach word meaning, rhyming, letter sounds, nouns, verbs, adjectives, adverbs, dictionary skills, punctuation—the list of possible skills goes on and on! You will find lengthy discussions of many language arts skills that can be taught through the use of poetry on the following introductory pages.

If children are exposed to poetry frequently they will not be frightened by the idea of trying to write their own verses. Suggestions will be given for starting such writing with simple poems that have specific patterns, such as "One, Two, Buckle My Shoe." There are numerous pattern poems that can be rewritten at different levels of difficulty by students of all abilities.

You will find that rhyme and rhythm are very important factors in most of the poetry selected for this book. The rhyme and rhythm are part of the attraction of poetry. The predictability of the words helps make poetry an important tool in teaching language arts skills to the non-readers, the emergent readers, and the independent readers in your classroom.

POETRY FILES

It has been my experience that students benefit from the opportunity to create their own poetry files in some way. Suggestions for creating such files will appear below. The advantages of keeping a poetry file are many. Students who have poetry files can reread their favorite poems during silent reading time or as an activity during small group lessons. A poem can be used as a copying assignment for handwriting. Individuals or small groups can practice and then recite favorite poems to their classmates. Some poems can be recited with such expression as to be "acted out." Other poems can be practiced and presented as stories or skits. Poems can be the beginning of some wonderful artistic efforts by your students as they try to depict an image from the poem of the week. Sometimes humorous, sometimes more serious, the poems inspire all kinds of expression.

Children enjoy learning poems and will delight in reading them again and again if they have easy access to the words. Here are several ways you might create poetry files with your students.

1. Classroom file:

Each week, as you introduce a new poem to the class, you will need to write it on a large sheet of chart paper or poster board, large enough so that students can sit together to see it, read it and share it, much in the same way as you sit and share a big book. Find a wall space big enough to put up "The Poem of the Week." It needs to be within easy reach of students because they may be writing on it or marking it in various ways with markers. You will probably want to mount the poem on a piece of poster board or heavy paper rather than right on the wall because the markers will go through the chart paper and you will have a mess on the wall.

Each Friday, as "The Poem of the Week" is shared for the last time that week, the poem should be mounted on tagboard or laminated and placed somewhere in the room so that students may reread it during silent reading time. The charts can be fastened to hangers and hung on a chart stand. Use skirt hangers, or else snap clothespins to fasten charts to regular hangers. It should be possible to hang all poems of the week on one chart stand. They do not require a lot of space, and you will see how much enjoyment your students get out of retrieving and rereading their old favorite and familiar poems.

HELPFUL HINT: By laminating the poem of the week, you will have a poetry chart that can be used year after year. If you will use water-based markers to circle, underline, and mark words during skill lessons, the marker can be wiped off, and the same poem can be used again!

2. Student poetry files:

Each student needs to bring a spiral notebook (8″ x 10 1/2″ size) to use as a personal poetry file. On a specific day of the week each student is given a copy of the poem to glue into the spiral notebook, or is asked to copy the poem of the week into his or her notebook. Students can then draw pictures to go along with their poems.

HELPFUL HINT: It is important to number the poems as they are put into the spiral

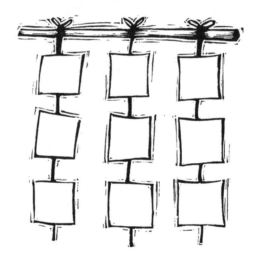

notebook. This makes rereading them so much easier. If poems are numbered, someone can suggest that the class read "number 17" and everyone can turn quickly to that poem and read together. If someone is absent on poetry file day, be sure that a copy gets put into his or her notebook.

You will need to decide which day of the week will

From *Daily Poetry* published by GoodYearBooks. Copyright © 1995 Carol Simpson.

be Poetry File Day, and then be consistent in this choice. There are good reasons to have Poetry File Day either early or late in the week. If you want your students to use their own copy of the poem on which to circle letters, underline words, and mark new vocabulary along with the lessons on the large chart, choose Monday or Tuesday as Poetry File Day. If instead you want your students to work only on the large chart with you in a group setting, choose Friday. The poem to be put in the file on a Friday will not be marked with circles and underlines, but it will be a clean copy. (It is my personal preference to put poems in our files on Fridays. We usually go back and reread poems, and I find it so much easier to read unmarked copies.)

3. Card files:

Older students might be given the assignment of copying the poem of the week on 4" x 6" file cards and then keeping their cards in a heavy duty envelope for easy access when needed. Illustrations will probably not fit on the file cards, so taking time to draw pictures may not be necessary.

HELPFUL HINT: When writing the poem of the week on your chart paper it is helpful to use markers of different colors for verses or pairs of rhyming lines. Your less able readers will find it easier to "Read the red words" or "Find a word in blue that starts the same as your name." Moreover, it is easier to read by colors when doing choral reading. The teacher can read the blue words, and the students chime in on the red words. Or, the girls read the orange words, and the boys read the brown words. Or divide the poem into four verses of differing colors and choose students to read each verse by color. If you are highlighting specific words in the poem for vocabulary studies, you might write those words in a different color from the rest of the poem. The level of your students and skills lessons will determine just how colorful your poetry charts need to be.

SCHEDULING POETRY

Once you begin teaching with poems, you will plan your own daily and weekly routine for using each poem of the week. Here is an example of a week-long schedule you might find helpful:

MONDAY: Introduce the poem, read it at least twice, and let the class join in if they are ready to read it with you. Discuss the poem's story or content. Share some related poems. Read a related trade book. Brainstorm a list of related thoughts or ideas on the poem's main subject. An example of this activity would be to list as many kinds of cats as you can, both fictional and nonfictional, if your subject is "cats." If your subject is "autumn," you might brainstorm a list of signs of the season's arrival, or changes that you must make in your daily routine because it is coming (example: wearing heavier clothes or turning on the heat). If the subject is "family," you might talk about what makes a family and how many family members live in your house.

TUESDAY: Reread the poem. Listen for, and mark, the rhyming words if appropriate. Find and mark words with specific vowel or consonant sounds, blends, digraphs, etc. This activity depends upon the readiness level of your students. Select a word from the poem that has a common word family (such as -ack) and then list as many words as you can that are also in that word family. How would you spell back, or shack, or track? Share another trade book. If there is time, you may want to try an extending activity.

WEDNESDAY: Do a choral reading, by parts if appropriate, or ask for volunteers to read aloud. Try a vocabulary study: find and mark any compound words, contractions, verbs, adjectives, adverbs, etc. You might also cover up a word and ask the class to replace that word with one of the same or opposite meaning. Try turning contraction words into the two whole words, read the poem, and discuss what happens to the rhythm if you make that change. Share another trade book. Try a writing activity.

From *Daily Poetry* published by GoodYearBooks. Copyright © 1995 Carol Simpson.

THURSDAY: Do a choral reading of the poem first, and then ask for volunteers to read the verses. Make a graph that shows some concept from the poem (example: draw and graph signs of Christmas coming), or do another extending activity. Share other poems on the subject, as well as another trade book.

FRIDAY: Read the poem for the last time. When hanging the poem, reread some of your favorites from weeks past.

WHAT CAN I DO WITH A POEM?

There is an abundance of learning that can be enhanced through the use of poetry. The following suggested techniques and activities are ways to do just that, but they are only a starting point, a beginning, something to get you going in using poetry to help teach reading and language skills. As you gain confidence in the use of poetry, you will come up with your own techniques that work for you, as well as your own list of favorite poems to share with your children.

You should find that your classroom becomes filled with print. A print-rich environment encourages rereading and writing because of the visibility and accessibility of many familiar words. Whether it be brainstorming lists, word family charts, stories children write, or the poems of the week, you will want to find space in your classroom to put up these words where children can easily find them, see them, and use them each day.

HELPFUL HINT: When and how you work with poetry in your classroom will depend upon the age of your students. Younger children enjoy sitting on the floor in a group as they listen to, read, and learn poems. Older students might feel uncomfortable sitting on the floor. Teachers may elect to have them remain at their desks or tables, and use the overhead projector in directing the learning activities.

1. Letter/sound association: This activity begins, if necessary, with young children searching in the poem for "the letter that looks like this" (the teacher would write and name the letter "c" or whatever the appropriate letter might be). The activity progresses to finding "a letter like the one you write at the beginning of your first (or last) name," and then to finding any letter(s) of the alphabet in isolation in the poem. Make a game of finding the letters in alphabetical order. Not all letters will be represented, necessarily, but when you come to a letter that cannot be found, you can write it beside the poetry chart

Using a spinner and cardboard, you can make a game of finding the letters. The child spins the spinner and must find the selected letter somewhere in the poem.

When children have mastered finding the letters, change the activity to finding a letter "that sounds like m-m-m" (or an appropriate sound). When children find the letter that makes that sound, be sure you tell them what the word says and stress the sound they identified correctly.

From letters you move to words. Following the same general progression, you can "Find a word that starts with 'r'" and then move on to "Find a word that begins like 'dog'" (or the appropriate sound). Ending sounds can be handled in the same way. "Find a word that ends with 't'." Find a word that ends like 'hat'." Add vowel sounds to your list of activities. Find a word that has the same sound of the letter 'a' (short) as in 'pad'. What sound is that?" Look at the spelling pattern (CVC—consonant/vowel/ consonant) which suggests that the vowel will be short. Find other words in the poem that have the same CVC configuration. Find a word with the same vowel sound as 'kite'. What sound is that?" Look at the spelling pattern (CVCe) which suggests that the vowel will make a long sound. Find more words in the poem that have the CVCe configuration.

As you can see, the study of isolated letters and sound associations are limitless. This activity can include blends, digraphs, prefixes, suffixes, and a host of other letter combinations. The activities that you do for letter/sound association will depend upon the level of your class. With each poem, you will find that the letter/sound association activity is listed first, but it is recommended that you do what is appropriate for your own class.

2. Rhyming words: Poetry is an obvious choice for teaching rhyming sounds and spelling patterns. The more children are exposed to poetry, the easier it becomes for them to hear intended rhyming sounds. When sharing a poem, be sure to stress the words that rhyme during early readings. As you read, provide the first of a pair of rhyming words, and pause to let your group chorus in with the second word. Read two lines and ask someone what the two rhyming words are. Locate the rhyming words on the poetry chart. Underline them and see if your students

can begin to recognize that most rhyming words appear at the ends of the lines. As you underline those rhyming words, take a look at the spelling patterns. For example, the words "puff" and "rough" rhyme, but are they spelled the same? What about the words "cat" and "hat," or other pairs. Identify those rhyming pairs that rely on two words instead of one ("spider" and "beside her").

As mentioned above, your emergent readers will find it much easier to follow along if the poem is written with different marker colors. Here is another reason for using markers of various colors. You can teach the rhyming pattern of the lines of a poem using markers and Unifix® Cubes. The rhyming pattern is the way in which four or eight or more lines of a verse are paired to rhyme. You may find that lines 1,2 and 3,4 rhyme. This is an AABB rhyming pattern. You may find that only lines 2,4 rhyme. This is an ABCB pattern. In the case of limericks, the first, second, and fifth lines rhyme, as well as the third and fourth, resulting in an AABBA pattern. When underlining the rhyming words, be sure to use a marker with a different color for each pair of words. Try to select marker colors that are also contained in your Unifix® Cubes set, if you have them.

When it is time to determine the rhyming pattern, look at the color of the rhyming word at the end of the first or second line. Where is the matching color located? Put together a strip of Unifix Cubes® that reflect the identical colors used to underline the rhyming words. Here is a 4-line example:

My snowman wears a hat of red

To keep the snowflakes off his head.

The scarf of brown will keep him warm

When winter brings another storm.

From *Daily Poetry* published by GoodYearBooks. Copyright © 1995 Carol Simpson.

Notice the rhyme in lines 1,2 and 3,4. Your students would underline the words "red" and "head" in the same color, let's say red. The words warm and storm would be underlined in a different color, perhaps green. When you are getting ready to determine the rhyming pattern of this 4-line poem, you will put together four Unifix® cubes, two red first and then two green. Children who come to you having done patterning in pre-school or kindergarten will be able to tell you that you have made an AABB pattern. By looking only at the words of the poem and talking about the marker colors that match, you are dealing with rhyme as an abstract concept. When you add the Unifix® Cubes to the lesson, the concept is easier to understand and becomes more concrete and visual.

Here is another verse to study and determine its patterning.

Oh, I'd like to go under the sea.

What a wonderful trip that would be.

I'd see fish and whales,

And clams and snails,

And I'd bring back a treasure for me!

Look for, and underline the rhyming words in like colors. If you will underline "sea," "be" and "me" in blue and "whales" and "snails" in red, you can then make a strip of Unifix® Cubes like this:

| red | red | blue | blue | red |

Your youngsters will see that it makes an AABBA pattern, not only because they can hear it, but also because they can see it.

When reading a poem that has lines that do not rhyme with the others, demonstrate the pattern by putting in a black and then a brown Unifix Cube® in place of the non-rhyming lines. For example, if lines 2 and 4 rhyme, but not lines 1 and 3, you might have a strip that looks like this:

black   red   brown   red

It is not difficult to determine the ABCB pattern of this verse because you can see it!

3. Word families: With each poem of the week you will find word families, or some words that fit basic spelling patterns. These are not necessarily the rhyming words in the poem. It will be useful to make word family charts to put up around the classroom. The purpose of the chart is to help students understand that words that sound alike are very often spelled the same. By changing the beginning sound, for instance, we can spell many words. Below is an example of a blank chart. Younger students would be asked, "How would you spell bake, shake, snake, lake?" and other words that fit this pattern. You might begin by asking your older students to think of words that fit the pattern. In either case, the student who names the word or letters that fit the pattern would come up and write the letter(s) in a blank space to make his or her word. If you hang these completed charts around the room, then, when a student asks how to spell a word, you can suggest that he or she find a specific chart and, in turn, ask the student what letter(s) would be needed with that spelling pattern in order to make the new word.

bake	_ake	_ake	_ake
_ake	_ake	_ake	_ake
_ake	_ake	_ake	_ake

From *Daily Poetry* published by GoodYearBooks. Copyright © 1995 Carol Simpson.

A spinner game (such as that pictured previously with alphabet letters) can be made using basic word families rather than letters. The student spins the spinner, a word family is pointed out, and the student tries to find a word in the poem, or name a word, that belongs in that family. You will want to use common word families, such as "-ack," "-in," "-et," "-og," "-up," "-ight," etc., on your spinner wheel.

4. Vocabulary studies: Some poems suggest the identification of sets of words such as colors (circle them with the color they name), or numbers (write the appropriate numeral on the word). Others offer the opportunity to find the names of the days of the week and number them 1-7. Circle the names of school days in blue and weekend days in red. Make a set of flash cards of the days of the week. See if students can arrange them in the proper sequence.

Poems often contain many descriptive words. As you work with adjectives and adverbs, see if students can illustrate or dramatize the meaning of the word. Try replacing descriptive words with ones of opposite meaning. Change "fat" to "skinny" or change "fast" to "slow." Use the cloze procedure (covering up or omitting a word in the poem, and then uncovering or writing one letter of the word at a time) to predict the descriptive word a poet used. You can do the same thing with verbs. "We jumped into the leaves" might be changed to read "We crawled . . ." or "We darted . . ." Omit the verb the poet uses and see how many verbs you can think of that would fit the context of the phrase. Write them on sticky notes and place them on the poetry chart in place of the original word.

Identify contractions and compound words and see if students can name the two words that were put together. When you identify two words for a contraction, write them on sticky notes so that you can easily place them on the poetry chart, or remove them. Read the poem with the contraction words in place. Put up the sticky notes with two whole words in place of the contraction. Read the poem

13

again. See if students can hear the change that often takes place in the rhythm of the poem. It helps if you clap or snap the rhythm as you read. Older students can be asked to try to explain what the problem is: that when two words are used in place of a contraction, there will be extra syllables which then upset the rhythm of the line.

Vocabulary studies can be used to teach dictionary skills. Take time to look up unfamiliar words in a poem. Try to predict their meanings using the context of the poem. Once you determine the meaning of a new word, use a sticky note to replace it with a more familiar word until the new word has been learned. Brainstorm a list of other words that mean the same thing. Other words that can be identified and studied would include nouns, proper nouns, pronouns, verbs, possessives, conjunctions, synonyms, homonyms, similes, metaphors, and others.

Emergent readers can be asked to "Find a word you can read." "Find words or phrases that are repeated in a poem. Find words from your spelling list for the week." "What is your favorite word in the poem?" "What is the hardest word in the poem?" "Find a word that means the same as _____." The kinds of words you might wish to identify go on and on. Of course, the words you ask your group to find will depend upon their readiness for the activity.

HELPFUL HINT: Whenever you are experimenting with new words to replace those on an existing poetry chart, use sticky notes. They are easy to put up and remove. This eliminates the chore of crossing out or trying to remove words on your poetry chart. If you laminate your charts, you can use erasable markers when changing existing vocabulary words. However, you cannot erase what is written on the chart before it is laminated. Therefore, you may want to omit the words you intend to study, leaving blank spaces instead, and then writing the missing words in place

From *Daily Poetry* published by GoodYearBooks. Copyright © 1995 Carol Simpson.

after laminating has been done. This allows you the freedom to experiment with many words and still present the exact ones used by the poet.

5. Dramatization of a poem: Let a group of students create a set of gestures or actions to go along with the words of a poem. They can then teach the motions to the rest of the class. Students can memorize favorite poems and then recite them for classmates. Students who recite poetry need to be taught to use a lot of vocal as well as facial expression. Brod Bagert has written numerous poems that are suitable for reciting with much expression. He refers to them as being "Poetry to Perform." He writes in an appealing child-like voice and with humor that children enjoy. You will find two of Brod Bagert's books *(If Only I Could Fly and Let Me Be.....The Boss)* listed in the poetry bibliography near the front of this book.

Many poems seem to tell a story that could be dramatized in a skit while the poem is read aloud or recited. Try this activity with familiar nursery rhymes first, to see if students can tell the story through actions. Once students see how easy it is to dramatize a poem, you can let groups of performers present a variety of poetic stories.

Let your students use the tape recorder and make a tape of an interesting poem. Perhaps they can add sound effects or soft music, depending upon the tone of the poem. Put the tape in your listening center and allow students to listen to their poems (and others') during a free choice reading time.

6. Reproduction books: Select an appropriate poem that can easily be illustrated using at least six or eight pictures. Assign pairs of lines (or in some cases, individual words or phrases) from the poem to the students and allow them to draw pictures for the lines, words, or phrases. Put the pictures in proper sequence, add the words of the poem, and then staple, tape, or bind the pages together into a poem reproduction book. Let your students take the "book" home and read it to their families.

7. Reproduction poem: This activity requires that you reproduce the lines of a selected poem on oaktag strips. Cut the strips apart (by phrases or individual words) and let students try to reproduce the poem by putting the words or phrases together in the proper order in a pocket chart. This activity can be used during free time or as independent work in a learning center, as well as a group activity.

8. Poetic word wall: I suggested earlier that you ask students to identify their favorite word from a poem. Select a wall space where you can put up mural paper of about a 4' x 6' size. Put a border around it and label it your "Poetic Words" wall. As your students find words or phrases that they like or find unusual, allow them to write them on this wall space. If you do not have the wall space available, put the words or phrases on flash cards and make them accessible for student use during writing times.

9. Creative writing: Every poem in this book comes with a story starter that you may choose to use with your students. You can also make up your own story starters. If you decide to write your own story starters, I suggest that you provide paper that is cut, or ready to cut, in an appropriate shape for the theme. Distribute plenty of these sheets so that students can continue to write and not be inhibited by having to use just one piece of paper. Then staple their stories together.

10. Rewriting poetry: Some poems seem to have a set word pattern that can be rewritten in various ways. The poem "Beans, Beans, Beans" by Lucia and James L. Hymes, Jr. is just such a poem. By replacing the adjectives and adverbs in the poem, you can change the main subject and rewrite the poem while keeping the original pattern. Thus a poem about "Beans, Beans, Beans" can become a poem about:

trees, trees, trees

or

shoes, shoes, shoes

or

books, books, books

or

friends, friends, friends

or

bugs, bugs, bugs.

On page 21 you will find a class rewriting of this poem with the "Bugs, Bugs, Bugs" title.

Poems with number patterns such as "Five Little Monkeys" (Anonymous) or Eve Mirriam's "Five Little Monsters," lend themselves well to rewriting. Try it using five little spiders, or five little turtles, or other animals of your choice. The popular nursery rhyme "One, Two, Buckle My Shoe" can be rewritten at any grade level. Students will determine just how difficult it becomes. The familiar "Roses are red, Violets are blue" has been used as a framework for writing numerous valentine messages. See how creative your students can be in composing their own verses. "Teddy Bear, Teddy Bear" (Anonymous) is another good poem for beginning writers to use as the format for their own rhyming pairs. If students attempt to rewrite the easy pattern poems first, they will be less fearful when it comes to writing other more difficult kinds of verses.

11. Comprehension: After listening to a poem, can your students remember its specific details? Can they draw a picture that represents the ideas suggested by the words? For a student-made bulletin board, hang your poetry chart and have the children make illustrations all

around it to serve as a border. Can they explain the poem in their own words? Ask the children to close their eyes and try to picture something the poet is describing. Try comparing and contrasting concepts in two poems on the same subject. Compare and contrast two poems by the same writer. With some poems in this book, you will find suggestions for making comparisons and contrasts by using Venn Diagrams. Here is a sample of such a comparison and contrast device.

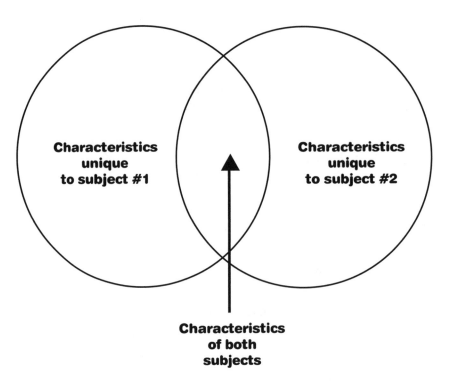

**Characteristics
unique
to subject #1**

**Characteristics
unique
to subject #2**

**Characteristics
of both
subjects**

12. Graphing a poem: Most poems suggest an idea for a graph. Whether it be a 2-line, multi-line, or a "yes or no" graph, you will find that graphing a poem is a fun activity for any age group. With some graphs, students will write their names on a graph line or color in a space. For other graphs, students will draw a picture (on 3" x 3" or smaller paper) to glue in place on the graph. Sometimes graphs are "real" and you will need to unroll a prepared grid upon which students can place real items such as shoes, lunchboxes, favorite fruit, or colored blocks. You will find suggestions for graphs of all types throughout this book.

From *Daily Poetry* published by GoodYearBooks. Copyright © 1995 Carol Simpson.

CLASS POETRY COLLECTIONS

Poetry collections can be kept and displayed in many ways. Here are two more ideas you might try. Be prepared to begin either of these at the beginning of the school year.

1. Poetry quilt: Each week, as you give a copy of the weekly poem to the students, you can also mount a copy on a poetry quilt. Very simply, this is a wall space large enough to mount mural paper that is 5' x 6' in size. Draw lines on the mural paper to divide it into 9" x 12" spaces. See the example below. Number the grid spaces (you will have 40), and glue each poem of the week on the grid

2. Accordion file: For this, you will need a sufficient supply of 9" x 12" sheets of oaktag or posterboard, on each sheet of which you will mount a poem of the week. Use wide heavy clear tape to bind the sheets together like an accordion or paper fan. It is not necessary to tape all of the sheets together the first week of school. Start with eight to ten sheets taped together and then add on as you study more poems. You will need to use the top of a long bookcase to display your accordion file.

HELPFUL HINT: You can use half the oaktag or poster board if you will mount poems on both sides of the accordion file. Instead of needing 36 to 40 sheets you will only need 18 to 20. You will also need less space to display this file. Remember to put a title page on your accordion file.

BEGINNERS WRITE POETRY

One challenge that students and teachers alike seem to dread is the writing of poetry. If students are exposed to a variety of poems and poets through the study of weekly and daily poetry, however, the job of trying to write one's own verses should become easier. Students will benefit from the experience of writing group poems, an activity in which they add only single words or small phrases to a coordinated effort directed by the teacher.

An example of a coordinated effort is this parody of "Beans, Beans, Beans" by Lucia and James L. Hymes, Jr. First-graders were asked to think of a kind of bug and a word that described bugs in general. With words in mind, along with the teacher's help, they wrote:

"Bugs, Bugs, Bugs"
by Mrs. Simpson's First-graders

Lady bugs, beetle bugs,

Ticklish climbing spider bugs,

Buzzing, flying bumblebee bugs,

Those are just a few.

Green bugs, brown bugs,

From *Daily Poetry* published by GoodYearBooks. Copyright © 1995 Carol Simpson.

Smelly red stink bugs,

Pesky crawling boxelder bugs,

Roach bugs too.

Big bugs, little bugs,

Don't forget tarantula bugs.

Last of all, best of all,

I like dead bugs!

The Fantasy unit contains a section called "Just Imagine." The poem offered for your consideration is called "Have You Ever Seen?" written by an anonymous poet. Taking this poem as an example, let your students write similar questions and then try to put them together into rhyming patterns. Some words may have to be changed or edited along the way, but students should be able to feel success in helping to write a really funny verse with this format.

For yet another simple writing project, you might try using the familiar song "Down By the Bay." Students can write their own lines for the part of the song that asks "Did you ever see a . . . ." The examples in the song include "a bear combing his hair?" as well as "a whale with a polka-dot tail?" The children can create their own questions by thinking of two basic rhyming words and then putting them together in an appropriate phrase. They love to sing the song when their own verses are included.

The "One, Two, Bubblegum Chew" poem by Meguido Zola, listed under "Colors & Numbers," is an excellent example of a parody of a popular poem. You can find additional parodies of this poem in other poetry sources. It would be helpful to find and share some of these other examples if you want your students to try their hand at creating their own parodies. Here is a sample:

1,2 'possum stew　　　　**3,4 eat some more**

5,6 stir and mix　　　　**7,8 clean my plate**

9,10 **eat again!**

A simple idea using a single letter of the alphabet became the basis for "A Poem" by Katie, who in first-grade wrote:

"A Poem" by Katie

B is for button.

B is for book.

B is for bathtub.

Look! Look! Look!

Katie's four-line poem reflects a very simple pattern that she constructed by herself. It could be imitated easily using other letters of the alphabet. Katie's poem shows that she understands the idea of rhythm and rhyme and where the rhyming words should be placed. Katie was pleased to share and teach her poem to the rest of her classmates. Everyone received a copy to put in his or her poetry file.

Kristy, a first-grader, recited a poem to her mother and got help writing it down on paper so that she could share it with others. Here is her poem:

Hold my Baby
By Kristy Mc G.

Hold my baby
Do not drop her,
She is fragel.
If you do,
She will cry,
If you do,
she might die!

Kristy was pleased to share her poem with the class. She, like Katie, understands how some poetry works to convey meaning with rhyme and rhythm. Both girls showed no fear of writing "poetry" because they enjoy it.

If beginning poetry-writing activities take place in an atmosphere where students are comfortable and find it easy to succeed, they will not dread the experience but rather look forward to its challenge and its fun. Remember to keep it simple.

MAKE A POEM INTERACTIVE

It is possible to make a poem interactive with moveable, changeable words and phrases. Such a hands-on poem needs to be written on large chart paper and laminated to make it sturdy. The interchangeable words must be written on oaktag strips and are held in place with paper clips. One half of the paper clip appears on the front of the chart and one half is taped in place on the back. It is necessary to cut tiny slits in the chart paper where the paper clips will be placed. Below is an example of a "Beans, Beans, Beans" interactive poem. It contains only the words that will remain unchanged in order to maintain the rhyme. See page 281 for an interactive color words poem.

Tennis	shoes	,	play	shoes	,
smelly	torn	running	shoes	,
			shoes	,

Those are just a few.

	shoes	,		shoes	,
			shoes	,
			shoes	,

| | shoes | , too. |

| | shoes | , | | shoes | , |

Don't forget [ ] **shoes** .

Last of all, best of all,

I like [ ] **shoes** !

TEACH SUMMARIZING

If you have never read chapter books to your emergent readers, give it a try! Select a chapter book that fits the theme of your weekly poetry lesson. Each day you need to read a chapter or two, depending on time constraints. Then ask two children to each draw a picture of an event that happened in today's chapter. When the children finish the drawings, ask the class to help you write something that happened in the story on each drawing. Hang each of the daily drawings in sequence on a wall space large enough to house all of the pictures necessary to tell the story on each drawing. Take time to reread the events represented in the drawings when new pictures are hung on the wall each day. This is a good way to review and it helps students understand that to summarize a story means to tell only the highlights.

When you have finished reading the chapter book, put all of the captioned pictures together to make your own book. You will want to add a cover and a comments page at the end of the story so that children can take the book home and share it with parents and get a written reaction to it. It is a book that takes much less time to read than the original , but one that children will enjoy explaining since all details are not written in the summaries on each page.

A FINAL WORD

This book presents many poems and related trade books and extending activities, including phonics and vocabulary skills lessons for your consideration. The order of their usage is up to you. They do not progress from easy to hard. Try some of the ideas in this book for a while, and when you feel comfortable using poetry to teach reading and language, you will want to choose some of your own poems and create your own activities that fit the level of your students. You need to select poems that you enjoy. That enjoyment will become evident to your students as you share with them the joys and pleasures of learning to read with poetry

MY WORLD

The poems in this unit are grouped together because they suggest a six-week study of the individuals in your classroom. The unit contains poems that deal with personal traits, families, behavior, favorite foods, favorite things about school, and favorite stuffed friends. This unit may prove useful early in the school year when you are trying to find out about your new students.

Before the class progresses through the activities, you may find it helpful to start a file or portfolio for each student that will contain written work as well as art and other projects that are done during this unit. Through a student's body of work, teachers can gain valuable insight into a student's likes and dislikes. The material also may prove helpful to show at parent/teacher conference time as a source of evaluation and assessment.

Everybody Says
by
Dorothy Aldis

Everybody says

I look just like my mother.

Everybody says

I'm the image of Aunt Bee.

Everybody says

My nose is like my father's.

But I want to look like ME !

OTHER POEMS ABOUT ME:

"Look At Me" by Ida M. Pardue (1)
"Quiet" by Walter L. Mauchan (1)
"Twins" by Jean Brabham McKinner (1)
"My Loose Tooth" by Ruth Kanarek (1)
"Friends" by Janet C. Miller (1)
"Me" by Walter de la Mare (3)
"Me" by Karla Kuskin (3)
"Mark's Fingers" by Mary O'Neill (3, 8)
"Stupid Old Myself" by Russell Hoban (3)
"If We Didn't Have Birthdays" by Dr. Seuss (3)
"I'm Nobody! Who Are You?" by Emily Dickinson (3)
"Insides" by Colin West (8)
"My Shadow" by Robert Louis Stevenson (9)
"I Don't Want to Shrink" by Robin Mellor (10)
"Collecting" by Jane Baskwill (12)
"If I Were In Charge of the World" by Judith Viorst (16)

BOOKS ALL ABOUT ME:

Quick as a Cricket by Audrey and Don Wood
I Like Me by Nancy Carlson
The Important Book by Margaret Wise Brown
The Mixed-Up Chameleon by Eric Carle
Bedtime for Frances by Russell Hoban
Mop Top by Don Freeman
Pajamas by Livingston and Maggie Taylor
Sam by Ann Herbert Scott
I Am Freedom's Child by Bill Martin, Jr.
I'm Terrific by Marjorie Weinman Sharmat
Shoes for Angela by Ellen Bartow Snavely
Arthur's Nose by Marc Brown
Arthur's Eyes by Marc Brown
Arthur's Tooth by Marc Brown
Wriggles the Little Wishing Pig by Pauline Watson
Leo the Late Bloomer by Robert Kraus
William's Doll by Charlotte Zolotow
Ramona the Brave by Beverly Cleary

From *Daily Poetry* published by GoodYearBooks. Copyright © 1995 Carol Simpson.

EXTENDING ACTIVITIES

Just as the poem suggests, "But I want to look like ME!" so the focus of this week's topic is to explore the individual characteristics of each student.

LETTER/SOUND ASSOCIATIONS: Letter/sound association work will depend upon the level of your students. If necessary, begin with playing the "Let's go on a letter hunt" game by finding the lower-case letters (except "c," "p," "q," "x," "z") in the poem. If your students are at a higher level, try going on a word hunt for "a word that begins like fish" or perhaps "a word that rhymes with rose." Use your own judgment and select letters, sounds, and words from the poem that fit your students' needs. There are four different sounds of the letter "o" ("oo") that can be identified in this poem. The short "o" sound is in "everybody"; long "o" is in "nose"; the double "oo" sound is in the word "look"; and the "o" in "mother" sounds like the short u.

RHYMING WORDS: There is only one rhyming pair of words in this poem. As you read the poem aloud for the second or third time, ask students to chime in on the last word of the poem and then see if they can tell you which word rhymes with "ME !" Underline the two words that rhyme. Look at the two different spelling patterns. One word has -e, the other has -ee. List other words that are spelled in this way.

WORD FAMILIES: There are many possibilities for word family studies in this poem. Two of them might be:

-ike (like, bike, spike, Mike, pike, hike, etc.)

From *Daily Poetry* published by GoodYearBooks. Copyright © 1995 Carol Simpson.

-ust (just, must, trust, crust, bust, rust, etc.)

VOCABULARY: Vocabulary studies in this poem could include "-'s" as used in possessives ("father's"), contractions ("I'm"), and compound words ("everybody"). If you do the contraction, try replacing the one word with two by putting sticky notes on the chart to cover up the contraction and testing the rhythm. The rhythm will become more obvious if you will quietly clap or snap as you read aloud. What happens to the rhythm when contractions are replaced by the two whole words they combine? Older students might explain that there is an extra syllable because of the alteration. Change the compound word into the two words that were combined to make one. This will not affect the rhythm, but it will demonstrate how we can put two known words together to form one word.

EXTEND WITH A BOOK: Share the book *Quick as a Cricket* by Audrey and Don Wood. After reading, discuss the animal-like characteristics that were suggested in the story. Ask the children how they might be like a particular animal. Each student can contribute a page of a class book about such animal characteristics by completing the following sentence in his or her own words.

"I'm as _____ as a _____ ."

Students can illustrate their sentences by drawing pictures or by finding animal pictures in old nature magazines. Combine the students' pages in the class book and select an appropriate title.

GRAPHING: Graph the many skin, eye, or hair colors that are represented among your students.

MY HAIR IS

BROWN **BLACK** **BLOND** **RED** **OTHER**

COMPARE/CONTRAST: Ask two students to come to the front of the classroom. Compare and contrast the two of them. How are they alike? How are they different? Try this several times as students get more sophisticated in their observations. Remember to try two students of the same as well as the opposite sex. Besides noting the fact that one is a boy and one is a girl, you could also compare and contrast hair and skin color, size, type of clothing they are wearing, shoes that tie or buckle or slip on, hair that is long or short, curly or straight, and any number of other ways to compare two people.

ART: Have students draw self-portraits, trying to include appropriate hair color and length, eye color, skin color, and kind of clothing worn that day. You may want to take a photograph of each student. Mount the self-portraits and photographs together on a bulletin board. Did the students draw some of their features accurately?

From *Daily Poetry* published by GoodYearBooks. Copyright © 1995 Carol Simpson.

LISTENING/TALKING/WRITING: Expose your students to the idea of interviewing someone by letting them pair up with a classmate and then ask questions to find out the other person's likes and dislikes. For their report, the interviewers should try to describe their person's obvious characteristics. They might also ask that person's favorite color, food, game, friend, and school subject. When the interview is over, the students should write a paragraph that describes but does NOT name their subject. The teacher then reads the paragraphs at random and, as hints are given in the report, the students try to guess who the interview subjects are.

BULLETIN BOARD IDEA: A nice way to feature each student in turn is to have a "Student of the Week" bulletin board. This becomes a place where the students can display their treasures, their baby and family pictures, and their best papers and stories. Classmates can write positive statements about the student who is being featured and place them on the bulletin board.

CREATIVE WRITING: Use the following as a creative writing activity: Look in a mirror. What do you see? Write a story or paragraph about yourself. Do you see freckles or a big nose? What color are your eyes and hair? Is your hair curly or straight, long or short? Do you have a nose like your father's? Do you look like one of your relatives? If you do not put your name on your story, can someone else figure out who your story is about?

MEASUREMENT: Cut a piece of yarn or string that is the correct length to equal the height of an average-sized student in your classroom. As each student is called upon, their classmates try to predict whether his or her height is equal to, more than, or less than the length of the piece of string or yarn. Try lining up all the students in order by size, from tallest to shortest or shortest to tallest.

PERSONAL HISTORY: Ask all students to try to bring in a baby picture that you can use to make compare/contrast statements. "I used to _____ but now I can_____ ."

When I look at myself in the mirror, I see_____

_____

_____

_____

_____

_____

_____

_____

_____

_____

_____

_____

Brother
by
Mary Ann Hoberman

I had a little brother
And brought him to my mother
And I said I want another
Little brother for a change.
But she said don't be a bother
So I took him to my father
And I said this little bother
Of a brother's very strange.

But he said one little brother
Is exactly like another
And every little brother
Misbehaves a bit he said.
So I took the little bother
From my mother and my father
And put the little bother
Of a brother back to bed.

From *Daily Poetry* published by GoodYearBooks. Copyright © 1995 Carol Simpson.

OTHER POEMS ABOUT FAMILY AND SIBLINGS:

"Mothers Are For . . ." by Dorothy Hewitt (1)

"Mothers" by Ruth Birdsall (1)

"Daddy's Steps" by Margaret Brown Elms (1)

"In Between" by Rose Cheroff (1)

"Brothers" by Muriel Lumsden Sonne (1)

"Sisters" by Muriel Lumsden Sonne (1)

"New Pet" by Lois F. Pasley (1)

"Six Weeks Old" by Christopher Morley (3)

"My Brother" by Marci Ridlon (3)

"Lil' Bro'" by Karama Fufuka (3)

"My Little Sister" by William Wise (3)

"These Are the Clothes That My Big Brother Wore"
        by Clive Riche (7)

"Snore-a-Bye Daddy" by John Kitching (7)

"Some Things Don't Make Any Sense At All" by Judith
        Viorst (16)

"The Even Trade" by Brod Bagert (20)

"For Sale" by Shel Silverstein (21)

"My Baby Brother" by Jack Prelutsky (22)

BOOKS ABOUT FAMILY AND SIBLINGS:

The Happy Hocky Family by Lane Smith

Jamaica Tag-Along by Juanita Havill

Sisters by David McPhail

A Chair for My Mother by Vera Williams

More More More Said the Baby by Vera Williams

Chicken Sunday by Patricia Polacco

The Pain and the Great One by Judy Blume

All About Sam by Lois Lowry

What Mary Jo Shared by Janice May Udry

Arthur's Baby by Marc Brown

Grandma by Alison Dexter
Island Boy by Barbara Cooney
Evan's Corner by Elizabeth Starr Hill
A Baby Sister for Frances by Russell Hoban
Amelia Bedelia and the Baby by Peggy Parish
The *Madeline* series by Ludwig Bemelmans
Weird Parents by Audrey Wood
Bigmama's by Donald Crews
Little Nino's Pizzeria by Karen Barbour
Sylvester and the Magic Pebble by William Steig
Nana Upstairs, Nana Downstairs by Tomie DePaola
The *Stupids* series by James Marshall

From *Daily Poetry* published by GoodYearBooks. Copyright © 1995 Carol Simpson.

EXTENDING ACTIVITIES

All families have disputes, and siblings always seem to be fighting. It is fun to take a look at how other families function. If we look at other families, both strange and typical, we can grow more accepting of our own differences.

LETTER/SOUND ASSOCIATIONS: All letters except "j," "q," and "z" can be found within the text of this poem. Emergent readers can go on a letter hunt to find and circle or underline them. Try using your letter spinner (spin and locate the letter that is pointed out) rather than doing letters in alphabetical order, unless that skill is needed. Find a word that begins with "b" or "br-". Find words that have a letter "i" and sort by long or short vowel sounds. Find words that have double letters ("tt," "oo") and discuss the fact that those two letters make only one sound, not two.

RHYMING WORDS: Find and underline the words that rhyme. Discuss the pattern of placement of rhyming words at the ends of the lines of print. Notice the common spelling pattern of the words "brother," "mother," "another," and then compare it to the different spellings of "said" and "bed." They rhyme but are not spelled the same. Make lists of other words with these spelling patterns.

WORD FAMILIES: This poem offers many word families for making lists of rhyming words. Two that might be used at this time are:

"-and" (and, band, hand, land, sand, brand, grand, stand, etc.)
"-e" (me, we, she, be, he, etc.)

VOCABULARY: Look at the words brother and bother. They are very similar in spelling, but different in the way they are pronounced. Find and underline all the brother/bother words in two different marker colors.

GRAPHING: Graph the number of people living in your students' houses or apartments.

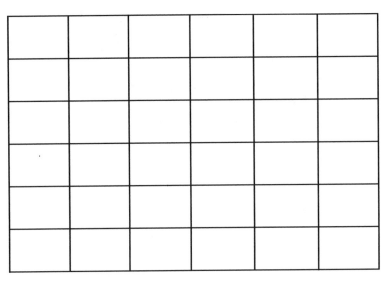

| 2 | 3 | 4 | 5 | 6 | or more |

EXTEND WITH A BOOK: Read one or more of the *Stupids* books by James Marshall and have the students compare and contrast that family with their own. List some of the things that make the Stupids an unusual family. What is the funniest thing that has happened to or in your own family?

SCIENCE: Look at possible inherited traits that students may exhibit. Skin, eye, and hair color are more obvious ones. But traits such as "hitch hiker's thumb" - one that seems to bend backwards when held up - or a "widow's peak" hair line are also possibly inherited. Do

From *Daily Poetry* published by GoodYearBooks. Copyright © 1995 Carol Simpson.

your students have straight or crooked little fingers? Are earlobes attached or free hanging? Is hair naturally curly or straight? Facial features such as a Roman nose or big ears may be inherited. Encourage your students to bring in family pictures so that inherited traits might be visibly identified.

CREATIVE WRITING: If questioned, most children have a favorite aunt or uncle or grandparent who does special things for them. Discuss some favorite or special people in the student's family and then have him or her write a story about that person. What do you do with that person that is special? Would you like to be like that person? Why? When you grow up, how will you be like that special person?

SOCIAL STUDIES: Make a neighborhood map of the streets and homes of your students. You might use a table top and make homes out of milk cartons or small boxes. Use shoe boxes for apartment buildings and your school. Make the streets out of construction paper. Label the streets by name and put numbers on the houses. The complexity of this "map" will depend upon the level of your students and how well they know their neighborhood. When students finish their "map" they can show how they walk or travel to school.

NAME _____

A very special person in my family is_____

_____

_____

_____

_____

_____

_____

_____

_____

Bubble Gum
by
Nina Payne

I'm in trouble

made a bubble

peeled it off my nose

Felt a rock

inside my sock

got gum between my toes

Made another

told my brother

we could blow a pair

Give three cheers

now our ears

are sticking to our hair.

OTHER POEMS ABOUT BEHAVIOR:

"We Must Be Polite" by Carl Sandburg (2, 14)
"Politeness" by A. A. Milne (2, 14)
"Let Others Share" by Edward Anthony (3)
"Rules" by Karla Kuskin (3)
"Manners" by Mariana Griswold Van Rensselaer (3)
"How to Say NO Politely When a Lion Invites You to Lunch" by Brod Bagert (20)
"Next Week's Angel" by Brod Bagert (19)
"Shirley Said" by Dennis Doyle (8)
"I Didn't Mean To" by Elizabeth Chorley (10)
"There Was a Little Girl" by Henry Wadsworth Longfellow (3)
"Table Manners" by Gelett Burgess (3)
"I Wish I Could Meet the Man That Knows" by John Ciardi (3)

BOOKS ABOUT BEHAVIOR:

N-O Spells No! by Teddy Slater
Ruby the Copycat by Peggy Rathman
Boris Bad Enough by Robert Kraus
Two Bad Ants by Chris Van Allsburg
Jumanji by Chris Van Allsburg
Weird Parents by Audrey Wood
No Tooth, No Quarter by Jon Butler
Alexander and the Terrible, Horrible, No Good, Very Bad Day by Judith Viorst
Dinner's Ready! by Jane Gedye
The Cut-Ups series by James Marshall
Benjamin and Tulip by Rosemary Wells
Angry Arthur by Hiawyn Oram
Miss Nelson series by James Marshall
The Boy Who Cried Wolf by James Marshall
Princess Smartypants by Babette Cole

From *Daily Poetry* published by GoodYearBooks. Copyright © 1995 Carol Simpson.

EXTENDING ACTIVITIES:

Children enjoy reading and listening to poems and stories about naughty boys and girls. Not only are the poems and stories fun, they also can be helpful learning tools. Learning about the wrong-doings of others provides a good starting point for further discussion about classroom behavior problems, actions that bother others or hamper learning.

LETTER/SOUND ASSOCIATIONS: All letters except "j," "q," "v," "x," and "z" can be located for letter recognition, if needed. The long "ee" sound can be found in several words in the poem. Take a look at short and long "o" sounds by finding the words "rock," "sock," and "nose," "toes." Then find numerous other words in the poem with the letter "o" and identify the sound the letter makes and why.

RHYMING WORDS: Locate the words that rhyme. Take note of their placement at the ends of the lines of print. Note also the spelling patterns of the words "nose" and "toes." Try to list other words with the same spelling configurations. Also look at the words "cheers" and "ears" because of the rhyming sound and differing spelling patterns. As the poem is read, be sure to allow students to fill in the second word in the rhyming pairs.

WORD FAMILIES: Two word families that could be presented from this poem are:

"-ock" (rock, sock, lock, block, shock. knock, etc)

"-ade" (made, shade, blade, grade, wade, fade, etc)

Put the word families on charts, as described in the introductory section of this book. Allow students to name words in the families and then suggest how they be spelled.

VOCABULARY: Two words that sound very similar but have different meanings are located in the last line of the poem. It needs to be emphasized that "are" and "our" are two different words. Be sure to pronounce them appropriately. One contraction word (I'm) is contained within the poem. Try replacing the one word with two (I am) and see what happens to the rhythm of the words as you read. The "ing" and "ed" suffixes are represented in this poem. Take this opportunity to work on verb tense. "Get" and "got," "make" and "made," "give" and "gave" can be distinguished as present and past tense with different spelling patterns.

ART: Discuss problems that can happen when gum is chewed in school. Most schools have a no gum rule. Why do you think this rule is so important to follow? Draw posters about this and other important school rules. Hang them in your school hallways where others can see them.

GRAPHING: Let students write their name on the appropriate response to the sentence on the graph.

From *Daily Poetry* published by GoodYearBooks. Copyright © 1995 Carol Simpson.

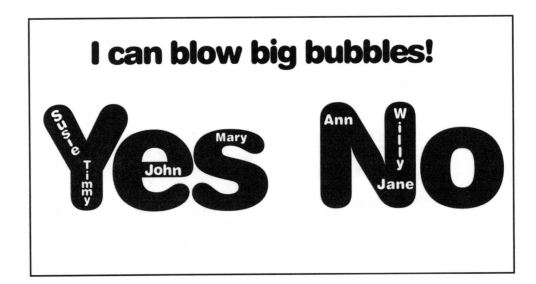

CREATIVE WRITING: Talk about problems with gum as well as other troubles students might have had with behavior, theirs or another's. Ask them to write a story that describes a problem and how it was resolved. Is there a difference between getting into mischief and being mean?

DRAMATIZATION: Invite individuals or a small group of students to memorize the verses of this poem or another poem about behavior. Allow the students to present their poems to their peers in a class presentation. Many of the poems suggested in this unit are written in a child-like voice that begs to be recited and acted out with much expression. Ask parents to come to your performance.

ILLUSTRATE THE POEM: Ask students to draw pictures that illustrate the events suggested in the words of the poem. Use small paper, about 6" x 6" size. Mount the pictures around the edges of the laminated poem and hang it on a bulletin board where others can see it.

EXTEND WITH A BOOK: Share the story of *The Boy Who Cried Wolf*. James Marshall's version of this tale is a good starting point for a discussion about telling the truth. Ask students to share times when they stretched the truth and what happened as a result of their actions. How would they feel if their friend told them a lie? Can you trust someone who tells lies? Write a class collection of little white lies.

Name_____

Once I got in BIG trouble when_____

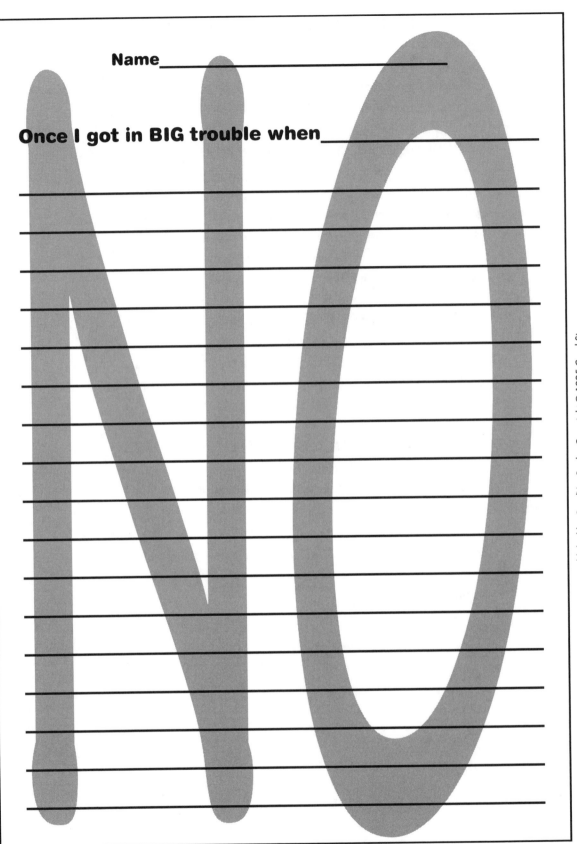

Beans, Beans, Beans
by
Lucia & James L.
Hymes, Jr.

Baked beans,

Butter beans,

Big fat lima beans,

Long thin string beans—

Those are just a few.

Green beans,

Black beans,

Big fat kidney beans,

Red hot chili beans,

Jumping beans too.

Pea beans,

Pinto beans,

Don't forget shelly beans,

Last of all, best of all,

I like jelly beans!

From *Daily Poetry* published by GoodYearBooks. Copyright © 1995 Carol Simpson.

"Beans, Beans, Beans" from *Hooray for Chocolate* by Lucia and James L. Hymes, Jr. Reprinted by permission of Addison-Wesley Publishing Company, Inc.

OTHER POEMS ABOUT FOOD:

"Morning Toast" by Doris I. Bateman (1)
"Celery" by Ogden Nash (1,3)
"Egg Thoughts" by Russell Hoban (3)
"Oodles of Noodles" by Lucia & Hymes L. Hymes, Jr. (3)
"Chocolate Cake" by Nina Payne (3)
"I Eat My Peas with Honey" by Anonymous (3)
"The Pizza" by Ogden Nash (3)
"I Like Soft-Boiled Eggs" by John Kitching (7)
"Pepper and Salt" by Barbara Ireson (7)
"Banana Talk" by Brian Jones (7)
"Spaghetti! Spaghetti!" by Jack Prelutsky (11)
"Cheers for Flavors" by Sonja Dunn (17)
"Butterscotch Dreams" by Sonja Dunn (17)
"Junk Food" by Sonja Dunn (17)
"Crackers and Crumbs" by Sonja Dunn (17)
"Hot Dogs Forever" by Sonja Dunn (17)
"Double Whammy" by Sonja Dunn (18)
"Recipe for a Hippopotamus Sandwich"
        by Shel Silverstein (21)
"Peanut-Butter Sandwich" by Shel Silverstein (21)
"Bleezer's Ice Cream" by Jack Prelutsky (22)

BOOKS ABOUT FOOD:

Growing Vegetable Soup by Lois Ehlert
Frank and Ernest by Alexandra Day
Gregory, The Terrible Eater by Mitchell Sharmat
Pancakes for Breakfast by Tomie DePaola
Wombat Stew by Marcia K. Vaughn
Peanut Butter and Jelly by Nadine Bernard Westcott
Bread and Jam for Frances by Russell Hoban
The Giant Jam Sandwich by John Vernon Lord
The Biggest Sandwich Ever by Rita Golden Gelman
Curious George and the Pizza by H. A. Rey

From *Daily Poetry* published by GoodYearBooks. Copyright © 1995 Carol Simpson.

EXTENDING ACTIVITIES

All children have favorite foods. Poems about food may be good teaching tools that lead to a discussion concerning our healthy/unhealthy diets. Here is an opportunity to learn about the basic food groups and what foods are important to include in our daily eating habits.

LETTER/SOUND ASSOCIATIONS: The letters of the alphabet are all included in this poem, except "q", "v," "x," and "z." Look at the words "chili" and "jelly"— two words that demonstrate that the long "e" sound at the end of a two-syllable word can but does not have to be spelled with a "y." Find and circle the letter "e" as it appears in words in the poem. Discuss whether the sound is long or short. Look at the word "few" and present the "ew" sound. List other words with the "ew" spelling pattern. The "th" sound of the words "thin" and "those" can be used to explain the two sounds of that letter combination.

RHYMING WORDS: Many lines of the poem end with the word beans. There is just one other pair of words that rhyme: few and too. Look at the spelling patterns of these words. List other words with -ew and -oo which have the same sound.

WORD FAMILIES: Two word families you may want to introduce and spell on charts at this time are the following:

"est" (best, nest, rest, test, vest, chest, crest, etc)

"ong" (long, song, wrong, strong, belong, etc.)

From *Daily Poetry* published by GoodYearBooks. Copyright © 1995 Carol Simpson.

VOCABULARY: Many kinds of beans are listed in this poem. Find and underline the kinds of beans. You might want to keep track of how many students have eaten each kind of bean. Some may be new kinds of beans to some of your students. Circle color words using the corresponding marker color. One contraction ("don't") and one compound word ("forget") are contained in the poem.

PUNCTUATION MARKS: This poem contains many kinds of punctuation marks that can be underlined or highlighted with markers and explained in context. The use of commas at the ends of many lines of the poem provide a good opportunity for explaining commas in a series: try writing the lines of the poem straight across a page instead of separating them on lines by phrases.

GRAPHING: Make a realistic three-line graph that shows how many of your students brought a sack lunch, how many will have hot lunch, or how many go home to eat. A large window shade with a three-line grid drawn with permanent marker will help students line up their graphing items as follows:

> sack lunchers" can place their lunch box on the grid
> "hot lunchers" can place a paper plate on the grid
> "home lunchers" can place one of their shoes on the grid

Be sure to discuss the results of the graph once it has been created out of real items.

From *Daily Poetry* published by GoodYearBooks. Copyright © 1995 Carol Simpson.

REWRITE THE POEM: Change the title from "Beans, Beans, Beans" to:

Sandwiches, Sandwiches, Sandwiches

Bugs, Bugs, Bugs

Trees, Trees, Trees

Shoes, Shoes, Shoes

Pies, Pies, Pies

Books, Books, Books

Some parts of the poem will remain the same, no matter what the title or subject.

"Those are just a few," the word "too" at the end of the tenth line, the "Don't forget" in the thirteenth line and the ending, "Last of all, best of all, I like_____," need to be left in place. This will allow you to write poems that rhyme in spite of the topic you select. See page 25 for a similar example.

SCIENCE/HEALTH: Do a study of the four basic food groups. Have students keep track of their food intake for a full day. Determine whether they have eaten foods from all four groups. Is their diet well balanced and healthy? If not, what foods need to be included that are not currently being eaten? On a sheet of large drawing paper draw a plate, silverware, and drinking glass. Draw pictures of foods that represent a healthy meal, or cut pictures out of magazines and paste them on the plate to illustrate a good meal. Cut lots of food pictures out of magazines. Sort them into the four food groups and then paste them onto large posters of the four food groups.

EXTEND WITH A BOOK: Read *Frank And Ernest* by Alexandra Day. Do your students understand the humor in restaurant talk? You may ask your students to make up their own food orders in restaurant talk and see if their classmates know what they mean by their order.

CREATIVE WRITING: Sandwiches are made using all kinds of meats and vegetables and condiments. Ask students to write directions for making their favorite sandwich creation.

MAKE A RECIPE BOOK: A student-written collection of recipes makes a great gift for Mom on Mother's Day. Read stories and poems about food and cooking, whether they be true recipes or ones that are strictly fictional. Each time you share such a book or poem, ask children to verbally list the ingredients that were needed. Write the ingredients on the board or chart paper. Then discuss the steps to follow when making that recipe. Demonstrate the parts of the recipe by writing the students' input on the board, whether it is accurate or not. When students seem to be comfortable with the parts of the recipe, ask them to go home and watch Mom or Dad as they cook. Instruct students not to tell the parent that they are writing a cookbook. When students return to school, ask them to write down the recipes as they remember parents making them. Combine all of the recipes in a class cookbook and then make enough copies so that each family gets a complete cookbook. Bind them with cardboard and cloth or Contact® paper, or laminate manila covers and bind the books in a spiral binding machine. These collections are guaranteed to be a big hit at home. Here is first-grader Ryan's recipe for a spaghetti salad that contains spaghetti, peas, and cinnamon applesauce.

Name **Ryah O.**   SPGate Salid

SPGate Pees . Sihamenaffal Sos.
Get Some SPaGate Cook It. then
Cook Some Pees. then Get Some
Sinamenaffal Sos. then mix to Gather
and eat.

SPaGate

Salid!

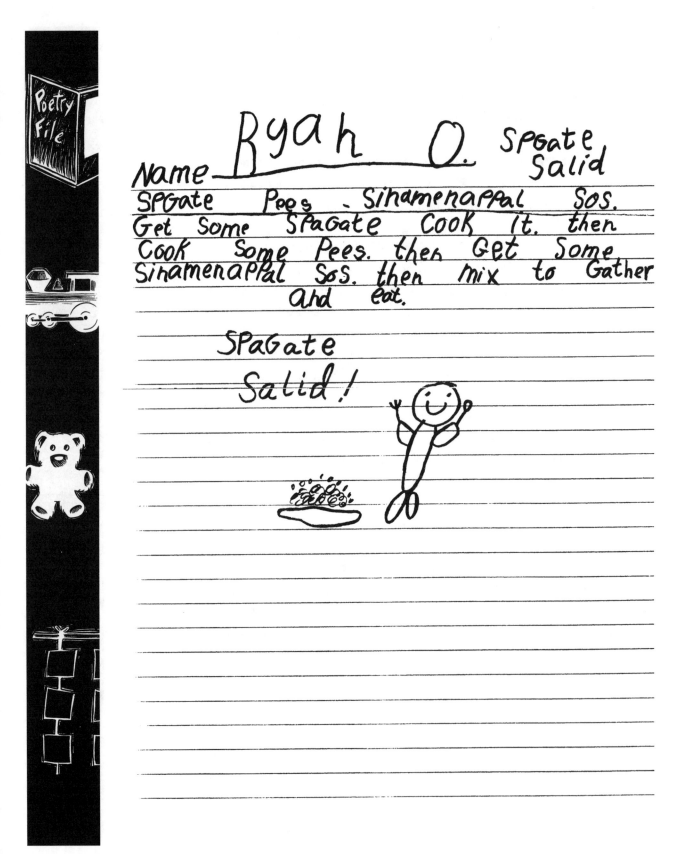

Name_____

I just created a terrific sandwich. Here's how you can make one too._____

_____

_____

_____

_____

_____

_____

_____

_____

_____

_____

_____

_____

_____

School
by
Winifred C. Marshall

School bells are ringing, loud and clear;

Vacation's over, school is here.

We hunt our pencils and our books,

And say goodby to fields and brooks,

To carefree days of sunny hours,

To birds and butterflies and flowers.

But we are glad school has begun.

For work is always mixed with fun.

When autumn comes and the weather is cool,

Nothing can take the place of school.

OTHER POEMS ABOUT SCHOOL:

"Back to School" by Aileen Fisher (1)
"School Again!" by Marian Stearns Curry (1)
"Now That I Can Read" by Ruth Etkin (1)
"When School Closes" by Dorothy M. Baker (1)
"My Teacher, My Friend" by Regina Sauro (1)
"The Marrog" by R. C. Scriven (3)
"History" by Myra Cohn Livingston (3)
"I'm Really Not Lazy" by Arnold Spilka (3)
"Yawning" by Eleanor Farjeon (3)
"Homework" by Russell Hoban (3)
"Homework" by Jane Yolen (3)
"Miss Norma Jean Pugh" by Mary O'Neill (3)
"Another Day" by John Cunliffe (7)
"Playground Count" by Julie Holder (8)
"School Break" by Joan Poulson (8)
"Teachers" by Sonja Dunn (17)
"Mean Teachers" by Brod Bagert (19)
"Homework" by Brod Bagert (19)
"Sick" by Shel Silverstein (21)

BOOKS ABOUT SCHOOL:

If You're Not Here, Please Raise Your Hand by Kalli Dakos
Somebody Catch My Homework by David Harrison
The *Miss Nelson* series by James Marshall
Never Spit on Your Shoes by Denys Cazet
Arthur's Teacher Trouble by Marc Brown
Morris Goes to School by Bernard Wiseman
Little Critter's This Is My School by Mercer Mayer
Ralph S. Mouse by Beverly Cleary
Teach Us, Amelia Bedelia by Peggy Parish
The Teacher from the Black Lagoon by Mike Thaler
The Principal from the Black Lagoon by Mike Thaler
What Mary Jo Shared by Janice May Udry
The Day the Teacher Went Bananas by James Howe
John Patrick Norman McHennessy, The Boy Who Was Always Late by John Burningham

From *Daily Poetry* published by GoodYearBooks. Copyright © 1995 Carol Simpson.

EXTENDING ACTIVITIES

Ask children about school and you will certainly get a variety of responses, some favorable and some not so favorable. Children have their likes and dislikes on the subject. Here is an opportunity to find out how your students feel about school.

LETTER/SOUND ASSOCIATIONS: In this poem, there are several words with "oo" that show both sounds of that letter configuration. Take a look at "school" and "cool" and compare them to the sound of "oo" in "books" and "brooks." The "tion" sound appears in the word "vacation's"; list other words with that ending. You can introduce the letter "l" as it blends with other consonants in words such as "clear," "flowers," "glad," and "place" to make a beginning sound.

RHYMING WORDS: Each pair of lines contains rhyming words at the ends of the lines of print. Look at the spelling patterns of those that are in the same word family as well as those that have different spelling patterns. "Clear" and "here" rhyme but are spelled differently. "Hours" and "flowers" are also spelled in different ways but sound alike. Make lists of other words spelled in those ways. The rhyming pattern of AABBCCDDEE can easily be demonstrated by using Unifix® Cubes of the same colors as the markers, as described in the introduction.

WORD FAMILIES: There are many word families suggested in this poem. Two that you might wish to introduce in context are:

-ool (school, cool, fool, stool, tool, pool, spool, etc.)

-en (when, ten, pen, men, then, hen, den, wren, etc.)

From *Daily Poetry* published by GoodYearBooks. Copyright © 1995 Carol Simpson.

VOCABULARY: It may be necessary to explain the word "brooks." Compare a river and a stream. Replace the word "brooks" with another word that everyone understands until the new word is clear to all students. There are compound words to find and underline. You might want to put a slash (/) between the two words that were put together to make the compound words. Find and underline the nouns that name school supplies, places, and things in nature.

KEEP A DIARY: Keep a daily diary of school events for at least a week or two. Each student can write in his or her own spiral notebook, or the class can keep a single diary that students can either write or dictate to the teacher. Write down what happens in school, as it happens, and include a reaction to the event.

PENPALS: Find another classroom of similar age and number of students. It might be a classroom in your own town or one that is not too far away. Let your students write letters to the students in the other classroom. Have the students tell about their own classroom and ask questions about their penpals' classroom. If possible, plan a picnic together with the penpals so that students can meet their new friends.

EXTEND WITH A BOOK: In Janice May Udry's book *What Mary Jo Shared*, a young girl has a difficult time selecting something to bring to school for show and tell. Ask students to describe a special show and tell item they showed once. Write a class collection of show and tell stories.

GRAPHING: Graph your students' favorite parts of the school day. Offer four to six subjects on the graph and ask the students to choose one. Students can write their names or, if available, paste a copy of their school pictures on the graph in the appropriate place. The subjects you list as possible choices will depend upon your own curriculum. You will need to decide whether to include recess as a part of the school day. Be sure to discuss the results of the graphing activity.

INTERVIEWING: Ask students to interview some of the adults who work in their school to find out what they liked or disliked about school when they were in your grade level. What made them decide to get a school related job? What kind of preparation did they need to get their job?

ART: According to the poem, when school starts the weather turns cool and autumn comes. Have the students draw pictures of the coming of autumn. Then make a class mobile displaying these signs of autumn. Use 3" x 3" pieces of drawing paper. The small pictures are fastened to yarn or string by pasting two drawings back to back, with the yarn or string being glued in between the papers. The example shown here will accommodate 18 pictures. Cut longer string and/or add another piece of string if you must include more pictures. The top of the mobile is a wooden dowel.

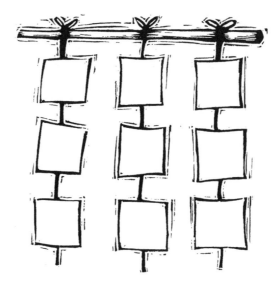

From *Daily Poetry* published by GoodYearBooks. Copyright © 1995 Carol Simpson.

CREATIVE WRITING: Assign the following topic for creative writing. What is your favorite part of the school day? Write a story that tells about it. Be sure to tell why you like that specific subject.

BRAINSTORMING: The poem lists just a few things that one needs for school. Brainstorm with your students a list of things they must go out and get in order to be ready for school to begin in the fall. Write a class book to which everyone can contribute a page that finishes the sentence:

"You know it is time for school to begin when ..."

SCHOOL

Name _____

The best part of the school day is

_____

_____

_____

_____

_____

_____

_____

_____

_____

_____

_____

Teddy Bear, Teddy Bear
Anonymous

Teddy bear, teddy bear, turn around.

Teddy bear, teddy bear, touch the ground.

Teddy bear, teddy bear, count to three.

Teddy bear, teddy bear, touch your knee.

Teddy bear, teddy bear, jump real high.

Teddy bear, teddy bear, touch the sky.

Teddy bear, teddy bear, put on a wig.

Teddy bear, teddy bear, dance a jig.

Teddy bear, teddy bear, pat your head.

Teddy bear, teddy bear, go to bed.

Teddy bear, teddy bear, turn out the light.

Teddy bear, teddy bear, say good night.

From *Daily Poetry* published by GoodYearBooks. Copyright © 1995 Carol Simpson.

POEMS ABOUT BEARS AND OTHER FRIENDS:

"Furry Bear" by A. A. Milne (2, 14)
"Grandpa Bear's Lullaby" by Jane Yolen (2,3,4,5)
"I Have a Lion" by Karla Kuskin (2)
"Last Word About Bears" by John Ciardi (5)
"Bear" by Jean Kenward (7)
"If" by Malcolm Carrick (7)
"The Land of Counterpane" by Robert Louis Stevenson (9)
"Teddy Bear Poem" by Judith Viorst (16)
"The Famous Purple Poka Bear" by Brod Bagert (20)
"Oh, Teddy Bear" by Jack Prelutsky (22)

BOOKS ABOUT BEARS AND OTHER FRIENDS:

Ira Sleeps Over by Bernard Waber
Bears (First Discovery Series) by Gallimard Jeunesse and others
Sand Cake by Frank Asch
Happy Birthday, Moon by Frank Asch
Mooncake by Frank Asch
Berlioz the Bear by Jan Brett
Little Bear by Else Holmelund Minarik
The Biggest Bear by Llynd Ward
Corduroy by Don Freeman
A Bear Called Paddington by Michael Bond
Where's My Teddy? by Jez Alborough
Blackboard Bear by Caroline Bucknall
Emma's Pet by David McPhail
Wake Up, Bear by Lynley Dodd
The Berenstain Bears series by Stan & Jan Berenstain
Big Bear, Spare that Tree by Jack Kent
Patrick and Ted by Geoffrey Hayes
Forgetful Bears Meet Mr. Memory by Larry Weinberg
Nobody Listens to Andrew by Elizabeth Guilfoile
Two Orphan Cubs by Barbara Brenner and May Garelick
Winnie-the-Pooh by A. A. Milne

EXTENDING ACTIVITIES

The main idea of this lesson, with its suggested poems and books, is to share stuffed animal friends. They do not have to be teddy bears. Children have all kinds of friends that are stuffed. They play with them, talk to them, sleep with them, and rely on them when the going gets rough. Encourage your children to share their best friends with classmates.

LETTER/SOUND ASSOCIATIONS: Go on a letter hunt for the lower-case letters of the alphabet, except for "f," "q," "v," "x," and "z." You have the opportunity to introduce the silent "k" sound, as in the word "knee." Try to list other words with the kn- beginning sound. Find the letter "u" and discover a variety of sounds it makes in words within this poem. The soft and hard "c" sounds are both represented ("count," "dance") and can be taught in context.

RHYMING WORDS: As you read the poem aloud, let your students say the second of two rhyming words while you pause. Most rhyming pairs have identical spelling patterns, with the exception of "high, sky" and "head, bed." List other words that contain these ending spelling patterns. Note the placement of rhyming words at the ends of the lines of print.

WORD FAMILIES: Two word families you might teach from this poem are:

-ig (jig, pig, wig, twig, fig, dig, etc)

-ay (say, way, tray, lay, gay, gray, sway, away, etc)

VOCABULARY: Each line of the poem contains a verb. Find and underline all verbs. Dramatize the actions these verbs represent. Try replacing verbs with other action words that have similar meaning. For example, replace "turn around" with spin around; "touch your knee" could be changed to tap your knee; or turn "go to bed" into hop to bed. Use sticky notes to cover up the original words with new verbs. Scatter the sticky notes around the poem and see if students can place them in their correct places.

REWRITE THE POEM: This poem is about a teddy bear. Ask the students to try writing a new poem about a sleepy dog or a fluffy cat. Do not change the verb phrases. Your new poem becomes:

Sleepy dog, sleepy dog, turn around.
Sleepy dog, sleepy dog,
touch the ground.

Or

Fluffy cat, fluffy cat, jump real high.
Fluffy cat, fluffy cat, touch the sky.

Instead of changing the animal, have the students change the actions to make a new verse:

Teddy bear, teddy bear,
bend your knee.
Teddy bear, teddy bear, come to me.

From *Daily Poetry* published by GoodYearBooks. Copyright © 1995 Carol Simpson.

Ask the students to rewrite the poem by featuring their favorite stuffed animal. Collect work from each student and make a class book of stuffed friends.

EXTEND WITH A BOOK: Frank Asch has written many books about a little bear. Share several of his bear books and then compare and contrast two stories using a Venn diagram format. Question your students about the bear. Would he be a good friend? Would you like to have the Frank Asch bear for a playmate? Why or why not? After reading several of the bear books, you might decide to write to Frank Asch and tell him what you think of his character. Have the students write down the favorable characteristics about this bear. Do your classmates share some of these characteristics?

SHOW AND TELL: Ask your students to bring in their favorite stuffed animals. They can show them and tell about them. Ask questions that stir the imagination, such as, "What is your animal's favorite food?" or "What is your animal's favorite story?" Children would love to believe that their stuffed animals are real, that they have feelings, and that they could come to life.

MATH: If and when your students bring their stuffed animals to school, see how many ways they can be sorted. Examples might be to sort by animal type, sort by size, sort by color, sort by texture, or even to sort by whether they are clothed or not clothed. Let your students suggest other ways of sorting. Line up the animals by size from the smallest to the biggest, or from the most tattered looking to the newest looking. If you have one available, use a balance scale to find animals that weigh the same: How many animals does it take to balance with the biggest one? Or how many pattern blocks or Unifix® Cubes does it take to balance with the smallest animal?

SOCIAL STUDIES/SCIENCE: Brainstorm a list of kinds of real bears. Look in nonfiction books to find out information about these kinds of bears. Locate their homes on a globe or map of the world. Find out what they eat, how big they are, and any other interesting facts you can learn about bears.

SELECT A MASCOT: For this activity, the teacher needs to supply several extra materials. You will need to select a stuffed animal to become a class mascot or friend. Allow the children to handle the animal. Have a contest to give the animal a name. Once the animal has become a "member" of the class, let the children take turns taking it home. For this you will need a backpack or duffel bag to carry it home. Inside the bag you will want to put pencils, erasers, colorful markers, a ruler, and a spiral artist's sketch book, besides the stuffed animal friend. Children then take the animal home over night and use the spiral artist's sketch book to write about the mascot's trip and draw a picture. When they return the next school day, they must bring back the travel bag full of materials, and then share what they did together by showing the class what they wrote in the spiral artist's sketchbook. Parents can write comments about the mascot's visit, also.

CREATIVE WRITING: Children love to pretend that their stuffed animals can come to life. Tap their wonderful imaginations by having them write stories about what their animals like to do. The story starter suggests a teddy bear, but they can change the subject to any animal they might like.

From *Daily Poetry* published by GoodYearBooks. Copyright © 1995 Carol Simpson.

Name_____

My teddy bear likes to _____

_____

_____

_____

_____

_____

_____

_____

_____

_____

_____

_____

_____

_____

_____

_____

ANIMALS

There are ten poems in this unit. All of them pertain to animals. It is possible to do the poems together in a ten-week study or to separate them into three smaller units: pets, wild animals, and animals of the countryside. Choose those animal poems that best meet your instructional needs and your students' interest. You will need to determine the length of time available and when an animal unit will fit into the curriculum.

Some of the animal themes lend themselves nicely to map studies and cooperative science projects that require studying animal characteristics and their habitats around the world. Should you decide to try one of the map/habitat projects, it may be wise to begin with it early in the week so that children have the necessary time to research and write about their findings. An important part of doing the research is the sharing of it with classmates.

Unusual Pet
by
Jane Baskwill

I just don't understand it,

When the kids all run and shout;

Every time I'm in a room

It begins to empty out;

I don't know why they scream so,

How come they're so alarmed?

Do you suppose they've noticed

This pet spider on my arm?

OTHER POEMS ABOUT PETS:

"Mother Doesn't Want a Dog" by Judith Viorst (3, 6, 16)
"I Would Like to Have a Pet" by Karla Kuskin (5)
"Notice" by David McCord (5)
"Barney and Fred" by Stanley Cook (7)
"The Gerbil" by Stanley Cook (7)
"There Was a Little Guinea-Pig" by Anonymous (13)
"Day Time Sleepers" by Brod Bagert (19)

BOOKS ABOUT PETS:

A Zoo in Our House by Heather Eyles
Can I Keep Him? by Steven Kellogg
The Boy Who Was Followed Home by Steven Kellogg
Buck, Buck the Chicken by Amy Erlich
Crictor by Tomi Ungerer
Dear Zoo by Rod Campbell
An Alligator Named Alligator by Lois Grambling
Do You Want to Be My Friend? by Eric Carle
Emma's Pet by David McPhail
A Boy, a Dog, and a Frog by Mercer Mayer
Just This Once by Joy Cowley
Little Critter's These Are My Pets by Mercer Mayer
Arthur's Pet Business by Marc Brown

From *Daily Poetry* published by GoodYearBooks. Copyright © 1995 Carol Simpson.

EXTENDING ACTIVITIES

Children have (or would like to have) pets of all kinds. This poem presents an opportunity to talk about pets, both common and unusual. Encourage children to speak up and share information about their pets. Children also need to listen to others as they tell about the care and feeding of all types of animals.

LETTER/SOUND ASSOCIATIONS: Find the letter "i " as it appears in many words in this poem. Discuss the long and short sounds of the letter. Both the hard and soft "c" sounds are represented in the words "come" and "noticed." The silent "k" can be found in the word "know." Words that have a final "y" ("my" and "empty") can be used to teach the concept that in a single syllable word with no vowel, the "y" has a long "i " sound, and if the word has more than one syllable the "y" sounds like long "e."

RHYMING WORDS: As the poem is shared and learned, cover up the second word of the rhyming pair and see if your students can remember what the word is. Point out the intended rhyming sound in the words "alarmed" and "arm." The rhyming words "shout" and "out" are more obvious.

WORD FAMILIES: Many word families are represented in this poem. Here are two that you might select for further study at this time:

"out" (out, shout, pout, snout, about, etc)
"et" (pet, jet, let, net, met, yet, vet, bet, etc)

VOCABULARY: This poem is an obvious choice for teaching several contraction words. Try replacing the contractions with the two words that were combined. Read the poem aloud, clapping or snapping softly as you read, and discover the problem with the rhythm when contractions are replaced with two words. Replace the word "alarmed" with one that is more easily understood by emergent readers. Ask students who do not understand the word to predict its meaning. If necessary, suggest that it means "scared" or "frightened."

GRAPHING: Make a graph of pets. Students can be given enough 3" x 3" pieces of paper so that they can draw a representative of each kind of pet they have. Choices should include dogs, cats, fish, birds, and "other pets." Some students will have more than one drawing to contribute because they have a dog, a cat, and perhaps a bowl of goldfish. Those who do not have a pet can draw a picture of one they might like to have.

EXTEND WITH A BOOK: Eric Carle's *Do You Want To Be My Friend?* is a colorful, mostly wordless picture book. The plot is very simple. A mouse is looking for someone to be a friend. One can easily tell the story of the mouse asking animal after animal if they would be a friend, and each animal in turn saying "No." Add dialogue to this story by cutting sticky notes in the shape of speech bubbles and placing them on the pages of the story above the animals who speak on each page. Children can tell the teacher what the animals might be saying. The words can then be written on the sticky notes and the wordless picture book suddenly becomes another easy reader for your emergent readers to enjoy. They will remember the dialogue because they wrote it.

From *Daily Poetry* published by GoodYearBooks. Copyright © 1995 Carol Simpson.

SOCIAL STUDIES: Brainstorm a list of do's and don'ts for pets and their care. Visit a pet shop and find out what unusual pets are available. Try to find out the responsibilities of taking care of unusual pets such as tarantulas or lizards.

SCIENCE: The poem of the week suggests a spider as a good pet. Many people do not like spiders. Ask the students why they think people do not like spiders. Brainstorm a list of spider attributes ("Spiders have . . . ." or, "Spiders can. . . ."). Which attributes make spiders scary? Look in nonfiction books to find out about the spiders that live in your neighborhood. Catch a spider and put it in a bug box with a magnifying lid. Look at it closely. Try to determine what kind of spider it is.

ILLUSTRATE THE POEM: Ask students to draw a picture of their arm. The poem suggests a pet spider crawling there. What else could crawl on your arm? Draw your scary pet crawling on your arm. When you read the poem, use a sticky note to change the word "spider" to tell what is crawling on your arm in your picture.

CREATIVE WRITING: Have the students write about the following subject. Pretend that the local pet shop is sending you a new pet. It can be a common pet or something very unusual. Without telling what it is, write a description of your new pet and let others guess what is in the box. Be sure to tell its size, its color, its eating habits, and what you and your pet like to play together. You might also include any sound it makes or unusual habits it has.

Name _____

I'm getting a new pet._____

What is it?_____

Monday's Cat
by
Meguido Zola and
David Booth

Monday's cat is full of milk.

Tuesday's cat is smooth as silk.

Wednesday's cat will roam the house.

Thursday's cat can't catch his

mouse.

Friday's cat licks clean her fur.

Saturday's cat just loves to purr.

Sunday's cat will scratch his head

and yawn and stretch and stay in

bed.

From *Daily Poetry* published by GoodYearBooks. Copyright © 1995 Carol Simpson.

OTHER POEMS ABOUT CATS:

"The Mysterious Cat" by Vachel Lindsay (2, 14)
"My Cat, Mrs. Lick-a-Chin" by John Ciardi (2, 14)
"The Lion" by Jack Prelutsky (3)
"Country Barnyard" by Elizabeth Coatsworth (3)
"Cats" by Eleanor Farjeon (3)
"Cat's Menu" by Richard Shaw (3)
"Alley Cat School" by Frank Asch (3)
"The Three Little Kittens" by Eliza Lee Follen (4)
"Confidence" by Martha Baird (5)
"Listening" by Aileen Fisher (5)
"A Cat May Look at a King" by Laura Richards (6)
"Tiger" by Valerie Worth (6)
"Tiger" by Mary Ann Hoberman (7)
"Our Cats" by Wes Magee (7)
"Letting in the Light" by Elizabeth Lindsay (8)
"The Lion and the Echo" by Brian Patten (8)
"The Lion" by Hilaire Belloc (13)
"My Cat" by Judith Viorst (16)
"Cat" by Sonja Dunn (18)
"Special Diet" by Sonja Dunn (18)

BOOKS WITH CATS OF THE WORLD:

Growltiger's Last Stand and Other Poems of T. S. Eliot
Cats (First Discovery Series) by Gallimard Jeunesse
and others
The Cat & the Fiddle & More by Jim Aylesworth
Cookie's Week by Cindy Ward
Here Comes the Cat by Frank Asch
Have You Seen My Cat? by Eric Carle
Millions of Cats by Wanda Ga'g
The Third-Story Cat by Leslie Baker
The Cat in the Hat by Dr. Seuss
Sam, Bangs, and Moonshine by Evaline Ness

Feathers for Lunch by Lois Ehlert
Who Is the Beast? by Keith Baker
The Fat Cat by Jack Kent
Sleepy Little Lion by Margaret Wise Brown
Tigress by Helen Cowcher
Green Eyes by A. Birnbaum
Fraidy Cat by Sara Asheron
The Cat's Midsummer Jamboree by David Kherdian and
Nonny Hogrogrian
Harry Maclary Scattercat by Lynley Dodd
Baby Leopard by Linda Goss
Socks by Beverly Cleary

EXTENDING ACTIVITIES

Every child either has a cat or knows someone who does. They all have had the experience of petting one or hearing it meow. Most will know about the cat's sharp teeth. Yet not everyone understands that the house cat belongs to a family of cats of the world that come in all sizes and colors and from a variety of habitats. Here is an opportunity to study the world of cats.

LETTER/SOUND ASSOCIATIONS: If needed, go on a letter hunt for all of the letters except "q" and "x." "Z" is represented in its capital letter form. The words "her," "purr," and "fur" offer the opportunity to teach controlled vowels. You can introduce the "ou" sound in the words "house" and "mouse." Try to list other words that have the same sound and spelling pattern.

RHYMING WORDS: There are rhyming words at the ends of each of the lines of the poem. Allow children to say the second word as you pause during a reading of the poem. Spelling patterns are easily spotted, except "head" and "bed." List other words that have these spelling patterns.

WORD FAMILIES: Two suggested word families to study from this poem are:

"ed" (bed, red, shed, fed, Fred, Ted, wed, etc)

"ill" (will, bill, spill, fill, hill, grill, still, etc)

From *Daily Poetry* published by GoodYearBooks. Copyright © 1995 Carol Simpson.

VOCABULARY: One obvious vocabulary lesson would isolate the names of the days of the week. Find and underline or circle all of the names of the days. Write the days on flash cards. Ask students to put them in proper sequence from Monday to Sunday, as they are named in the poem. Use this poem to teach the 's possessive. Compare the function of the apostrophe in "Monday's" with the one in the word "can't."

DRAMATIZE THE POEM: The lines of this poem suggest actions that could be dramatized as the poem is recited. The phrase "full of milk" might suggest rubbing ones tummy. "Smooth as silk" could mean petting one's arm. And "roam the house" could mean moving one's hands as if walking. Each line could have its own motion. Doing the motions is not only fun for emergent readers, it also helps reinforce the words of the poem.

SCIENCE/SOCIAL STUDIES: Brainstorm a list of cats of all kinds, both real and fictional story or cartoon characters. Write the names of the suggested cats on flash cards. Sort the names into two categories: real and fictional. Let small groups of students work together to find out information about some of the real cats listed in the brainstorming process. Learn about habitat, eating habits, and size of the cats selected. Information gained in research should be shared with classmates. Through the use of a Venn diagram, compare and contrast a real cat and a fictional character. How are they alike and different?

GRAPHING: Students can color in a space on a graph to indicate their favorite big cat. Choices should be limited to four or five (lion, tiger, cheetah, jaguar, leopard, bobcat to name a few).

LION					
TIGER					
CHEETAH					
JAGUAR					

EXTEND WITH A BOOK: Read *Have You Seen My Cat?* by Eric Carle. As the cats of the world are pictured in the story, take an around-the-world journey on a map or globe and show the origin of each of the animals. You will travel to numerous places around the world in doing this activity. For many youngsters, it will be an informative journey as they discover that lions and tigers do not live in the same part of the world.

CREATIVE WRITING: The story of *Cookie's Week* by Cindy Ward follows the days-of-the-week pattern in the poem by taking us on a day-to-day adventure with Cookie, a kitty. This story suggests that Cookie does not sleep all day while the master is away. Put your students' creative imaginations to work writing stories about what their kitty (real or pretend) does all day while they are in school. Put the stories together in a class collection that might be called *Kitty's Day*. The pattern of *Cookie's Week* makes it an easy story to parody.

From *Daily Poetry* published by GoodYearBooks. Copyright © 1995 Carol Simpson.

SHOW AND TELL: Although you are not encouraged to have everyone's kitty come to school on the same day, you might consider asking mothers if they could bring them in on different days during your one-week study of cats. The child whose cat is coming to school can show and tell about their pet.

Name_____

**While I'm away all day
my kitty**_____

_____

_____

_____

_____

_____

_____

_____

_____

_____

_____

_____

_____

_____

_____

_____

Dogs
by
John Kitching

Dogs big, dogs small

Dogs short, dogs tall

Dogs fat, dogs thin

Dogs that make a dreadful din

Dogs smooth, dogs hairy

Dogs friendly, dogs scary

Dogs brown, dogs white

Dogs that bark all through the night.

Dogs that run, dogs that walk

Dogs that make you think they'll talk,

Dogs awake, dogs asleep

Dogs for the blind, dogs for the sheep.

The best of all the dogs I know

Goes with me everywhere I go.

POEMS ABOUT DOGS:

"My Dog" by Helen Lorraine (1)
"Dogs" by Marchette Chute (2, 14)
"The Hairy Dog" by Herbert Asquith (3)
"Lone Dog" by Irene McLeod (3)
"I've Got a Dog" by Anonymous (3, 13)
"Vern" by Gwendolyn Brooks (5)
"My Dog" by Vernon Scannell (8)
"There Was a Little Dog" by Anonymous (13)
"Wiggle Waggle, Wiggle Waggle" by Anonymous (13)
"My Dog Jay" by Sonja Dunn (18)
"My Dog, He Is an Ugly Dog" by Jack Prelutsky (22)

BOOKS ABOUT DOGS:

The Mystery of the Stolen Blue Paint by Steven Kellogg
Arthur's New Puppy by Marc Brown
Fido by Stephanie Calmenson
Who Wants Arthur? by Amanda Graham
Harry Maclary from Donaldson's Dairy by Lynley Dodd
Harry Maclary's Bone by Lynley Dodd
The Puppy Who Wanted a Boy by Jane Thayer
Harry the Dirty Dog by Gene Zion
The *Ribsy* series by Beverly Cleary
The *Clifford* series by Norman Bridwell
Whistle for Willie by Ezra Jack Keats
Two Dog Biscuits by Beverly Cleary
Angus and the Ducks by Marjorie Flack
Don't Frighten the Lion by Margaret Wise Brown
The *Pinkerton* series by Steven Kellogg
Freckles & Willie by Margery Cuyler
The Perfect Ride by Lady McCrady
Jack and the Puppy by Jane Burton
Harry and the Lady Next Door by Gene Zion
No Roses for Harry by Gene Zion
A Dog Called Kitty by Bill Wallace
Where's Spot? by Eric Hill

From *Daily Poetry* published by GoodYearBooks. Copyright © 1995 Carol Simpson.

EXTENDING ACTIVITIES

Encourage your students to use first-hand information they have gained from experiences with dogs at home or in their neighborhood in order to discuss tricks dogs can do, good or bad manners they exhibit, and what they like to play.

LETTER/SOUND ASSOCIATIONS: If you are still going on a letter hunt you will find all letters except "q," "x," and "z" in this poem. The letter "j" is in capital form only. All five short vowel sounds are included in the words of this poem. All five long vowel sounds can also be found. See if your students can find and underline a word for each of the ten vowel sounds ("fat," "best," "big," "dog," "run," "make," "me," "white," "go," "through"). Use this poem to present the "ch," "wh," "sh," and "th" sounds.

RHYMING WORDS: Some of the rhyming pairs present differing spelling patterns even though the sounds are the same. Look at "hairy" and "scary," "white" and "night," and "know" and "go." Present lists of other words that have these spelling patterns. Take note of the placement of rhyming words at the ends of lines of print. You may want to begin presenting the idea of an AABB rhyming pattern found in the four-line verses of this poem.

WORD FAMILIES: Two families you might choose to present and put on charts are:

"og" (dog, hog, log, fog, frog, bog, etc.)

"eep" (sheep, sleep, deep, cheep, sweep, weep, etc.)

VOCABULARY: Before your poem is ever read aloud, you might want to cover up the word "din" with a sticky note. Write the word "noise" on the sticky note. Explain to the children that a word that means the same as "noise" is in the poem. Give a clue to the identity of the word (it begins with "d" and it rhymes with "thin") in order to have the word named. Each time the poem is read, remind students that the word "din" means noise. By the end of the week, they will understand the new word. Find all of the adjectives that describe the dogs in the poem. Circle color words with the appropriate color marker.

BRAINSTORMING: Write names of kinds of dogs on a piece of chart paper as students call them out. Select two familiar kinds of dogs, such as a Dalmatian and a Collie. Display a good picture of each, if available, and compare and contrast the characteristics of each kind.

SORTING & SEQUENCING: Provide students with an assortment of pictures of dogs. Sort them by size, color, length of fur, and other attributes. Sequence them from smallest to biggest.

CREATIVE WRITING: Every child knows that you can teach dogs to do tricks. Ask the students to think of a good trick they might teach their dog (or their neighbor's dog). Then ask them to write a story that tells the steps they would need to take in teaching the dog this neat new trick. If possible, have them test the new trick on the dog. Does it work? Have them share their experiences at teaching the dog a new trick.

From *Daily Poetry* published by GoodYearBooks. Copyright © 1995 Carol Simpson.

MANNERS: Unless they have been trained, dogs like to lick people in the face and smell them to get to know them. Some people consider these gestures to be bad manners and are not pleased. Brainstorm a list of bad manners your students' dogs (or neighbor's dog) display. Draw pictures of these bad manners and label them with sentences that tell what the dogs are doing (chasing cars, digging in the neighbor's garden, etc.). Put the pictures and sentences together in a class book about bad manners. Be sure to read the class book together and share it with others. Allow your students to take the book home to read with their families.

SHOW AND TELL: As with cats, it is better if the dogs that come to visit your classroom for show and tell do not come on the same day. Try to schedule the animal visits at different times. As the dogs come to visit, their owners can show and tell about them. If the student is in the process of teaching a new trick, be sure the class gets to see the progress being made in learning it.

EXTEND WITH A BOOK: Read the book *Fido* by Stephanie Calmenson. This book suggests that dogs and their owners can sometimes look alike. What attributes do the dog and owner share? Compare and contrast the two. Do your students and their dogs look alike, too?

ILLUSTRATE THE POEM: This poem describes dogs in a multitude of ways (big, small, short, tall, fat, thin, etc.). Draw pictures that show the different ways dogs are described. If you prefer, look for dog pictures in old magazines. Cut them out and glue them onto or around the edges of the poetry chart. As the poem suggests, some dogs have work to do. There are dogs who help the blind and dogs who tend and herd sheep. What other dogs can you find that work for people?

PLACE VALUE: Draw a very large Dalmation on white paper. Give it many spots. Ask your children to guess how many spots are on the dog's body. Write down all guesses. Count the actual number of spots by circling groups of ten, again and again, until there are only ones left. Count the tens and ones and find out the exact number of spots on the dog. Award a prize to the person who came the closest to guessing the correct number.

Name _____

If I could teach my dog a new trick it would be _____

_____

_____

_____

_____

_____

_____

_____

_____

_____

_____

_____

_____

_____

_____

_____

I Went To The Animal Fair
Anonymous

I went to the animal fair,

The birds and beasts were there.

The big baboon by the light of the moon

Was combing his auburn hair.

The monkey he got drunk,

He stepped on the elephant's trunk.

The elephant sneezed

And fell on his knees,

And that was the end of the monk,

the monk, the monk.

And that was the end

of the monk.

OTHER POEMS ABOUT THE ZOO:

"At the Zoo" by Lena B. Ellingwood (1)
"Will You?" by Eve Merriam (4)
"Wouldn't It Be Funny?" by Pixie O'Harris (5)
"At the Zoo" by Judith Nicholls (8)

BOOKS ABOUT THE ZOO:

Jungle Animals (Eye Openers series) by Angela Royston
Zoo Animals by Sandy Cortright
Zoo Babies by Miriam Morton
Zoo Animals by Cathy Kilpatrick
Searchin' Safari by Jeff O'Hare
Whose Toes Are Those? A Peep Hole Story by Joyce Elias
Curious George Visits the Zoo by H. A. Rey
Zoophabets by Robert Tallon
Dear Zoo by Rod Campbell
At the Zoo by Paul Simon
Who's in the Shed? by Brenda Parkes
Just So Stories by Rudyard Kipling

EXTENDING ACTIVITIES

In many elementary classrooms, a unit in which children study the zoo and wild animals is very popular. Here is an opportunity to introduce your zoo lesson with poetry. The poem for this week is always a favorite in the elementary classroom. It will be one of those that your students will ask to read over and over again because of the humor. You can also teach the tune since this poem is really a song.

LETTER/SOUND ASSOCIATIONS: You may want to try your spinner games as described in "How to Use This Book" (page 1). Let students spin to find both individual letters and word families because many are represented in this poem. There are opportunities to study the vowel sound of "oo" (as in moon). You might choose to look at the silent "b" in the word combing. You will find the "th" sound present in many words. Look at the word "elephant" and discover that "ph" makes the sound of the letter "f." Try to list other words with the "ph" spelling pattern.

RHYMING WORDS: Locate and underline with like colors the three words that rhyme in each verse. Take note of differing spelling patterns in words such as "fair" and "there." The verses have rhyming words at the ends of the first, second, and fifth lines of the poem. Use your Unifix® Cubes to illustrate the AABCA rhyming pattern of the poem.

From *Daily Poetry* published by GoodYearBooks. Copyright © 1995 Carol Simpson.

WORD FAMILIES: Two families you might choose to teach at this time through charting are:

"in" (in, win, fin, din, pin, spin, chin, etc.)

"ent" (went, sent, bent, dent, spent, Kent, extent, etc.)

VOCABULARY: You may want to identify the names of all the animals in the poem. The anonymous poet names birds—which even the youngest listener can understand and locate in a picture. What about the "beasts"—what do your students think the poet means by this word? What color is auburn?

SCIENCE: Brainstorm a lengthy list of zoo animals. Write them on flash cards. Students can then sort the animal names into groups such as cats, primates, reptiles, fowl, sea animals, and "other" mammals. Discuss the attributes that help you determine into which group you want to place animal names. Find posters of as many zoo animals as you can, both common ones and lesser known ones, and display them around your classroom. By the end of your animal studies, your students may be able to identify all of them by name and indicate the groups to which they belong.

CREATIVE WRITING: If possible, take a field trip to a local zoo. Prior to the trip, prepare your students by talking about, and showing pictures of, animals they will be seeing. Ask them to imagine trading places with an animal in the zoo. Which animal would you like to be and why? Write a story about yourself as an animal in the zoo.

MAKE A CLASS BOOK: A peep hole book is fun to do with zoo animals. Try to get a collection of *World (National Geographic)* or *Ranger Rick* or some other nature magazines. Find some that contain photographs of animals of all kinds. Allow each student the opportunity to select one large picture to mount on a piece of 12" x 18" construction paper. The name of the animal can be written on the page. The preceding page should be one that is specially prepared by the teacher. The words on the preceding page might say, "Guess what Julie (or any child's name) saw." The page should have a small peep hole cut very carefully to show only a small portion of the animal pictured on the next page. The hole should provide just enough of a peek to get ideas flowing about which animal might be on the next page. Carefully put all the pages together with binding rings so that you have a class peephole book. Children will delight in predicting what is coming on the next page. After they have looked at the book several times they will know the answers quite well. They will enjoy saying "Guess what _____ saw" out loud. And finding the name of every classmate in the book, especially if they take the book home to share with their families. To make the project more difficult for your better readers, ask them to write clues to their animal's identity on the preceding page and to write complete sentences or more on the page with the animal picture.

EXTEND WITH A BOOK: The book *Dear Zoo* by Rod Campbell is an enjoyable story to parody. After reading the book, talk about the pattern contained in its pages. Give each student a large sheet of drawing paper. and ask them to draw a picture of a zoo animal they might like to have for a pet. When a page is finished, the teacher or student covers the animal picture with a lift-up flap which becomes a crate when lines are added. Add text that is similar in pattern to the original book. Share your class book with others. Let your students check out the book and take it home to share with families.

From *Daily Poetry* published by GoodYearBooks. Copyright © 1995 Carol Simpson.

GRAPHING: Have each student color or write his or her name in a space on the graph to show a response to the question asked.

HAVE YOU EVER BEEN TO THE ZOO?				
YES				
NO				

ART PROJECT: Give each child a large sheet of drawing paper. Let them draw a zoo animal of their choice. When the picture is done, glue black strips to the drawing to represent the bars of a cage. Add wheels to the bottom, put all of the drawings in a row, add an "engine" and call it a zoo train.

A-B-C'S OF ANIMALS: Look in encyclopedias and dictionaries to find a list of 26 animal names, enough for one beginning with each letter of the alphabet. Some letters are very tough, but it is possible to find them. Find an alphabet strip (the kind you hang up in your classroom for handwriting and letter recognition) that has animal pictures on it. You can probably find all 26 words you will need on such an alphabet strip. Write the animal names in random order on the board or large chart paper. Ask your students to write them in alphabetical order on lined paper.

THE ZOO

Name _____

I'd like to be an animal in the zoo.
I'd like to trade places with

_____
_____
_____
_____
_____
_____
_____
_____
_____
_____
_____
_____

The Elephant
by
Arnold Sundgaard

The elephant is quite a beast,

He's rather large to say the least,

And though his size is most impressive

The elephant is not aggressive,

He never throws his weight around,

Still he always holds his ground.

He only wants to feel secure.

Long may the elephant endure!

OTHER POEMS ABOUT ELEPHANTS:

"Eletelephony" by Laura E. Richards (2,3, 14)
"Holding Hands" by Lenore M. Link (3)
"Oliphaunt" by J. R. R. Tolkien (3)
"Beside the Line of Elephants" by Edna Becker (3)
"The Handiest Nose" by Aileen Fisher (4)
"Cradle Song of the Elephants" by Adriano delValle (5)
"Circus Elephant" by Kathryn Worth (7)
"Elephantastic" by Michael Johnson (10)
"The Elephant" by Hilaire Belloc (13)
"I Toss Them to My Elephant" by Jack Prelutsky (22)

BOOKS ABOUT ELEPHANTS:

The Trouble with Elephants by Chris Riddell
The Right Number of Elephants by Jeff Shepard
Forgetful Bears Meet Mr. Memory by Larry Weinberg
Too Many Mice by Barbara Brenner
Oliver by Syd Hoff
Frank and Ernest by Alexandra Day
The Story of Babar by Jean de Brunhoff
Elephants Aloft by Kathi Appelt

From *Daily Poetry* published by GoodYearBooks. Copyright © 1995 Carol Simpson.

EXTENDING ACTIVITIES

Children love elephants because of their massive size and wonderful trunks. Any visit to a zoo would be incomplete without stopping to feed some peanuts to those amazing giants, or watching them squirt water with their trunks. There is much information about elephants to be found in nonfiction materials. Here is an opportunity to examine the differences between African and Indian elephants.

LETTER/SOUND ASSOCIATIONS: This poem of the week is one of the few that contains the letter "q," although "j," "k," and "x" are not present. Use the words "impressive" and "aggressive" to teach double consonants. The "ph" (f) sound can be taught also. There are examples of the "ou" and "ow" sounds; teach the students to practice trying each of the two possible sounds they make when determining which one is correct in a particular word.

RHYMING WORDS: All rhyming words in this poem have like spelling patterns. Take note of the placement of the rhyming words at the ends of the lines of print. Note the AABBCCDD rhyming pattern of the lines.

WORD FAMILIES: There are numerous word families that could be taught and charted in this poem. Two common ones you might want to choose are:

"ow" (throw, show, slow, grow, snow. tow, bow, etc.)

"ot" (not, lot, got, pot, rot, cot, spot, clot, etc.)

VOCABULARY: The words "secure" and "endure" will probably need to be introduced as meaning "safe" and "last for a long time." You may also want to explain the words "impressive" and "aggressive." If necessary, cover the new words with sticky notes that have words that are more familiar until the new words are better understood. There are phrases in the poem that will need interpretation and explanation as well, such as "throws his weight around" and "holds his ground." The message in the poem is clearer when everyone agrees upon what these phrases mean.

COMPARE/CONTRAST: List the attributes of an elephant. Compare his trunk to a hose, his strength to a bulldozer, and other similes. Put pages together to make a class book about elephants by having the students complete the following sentence:

An elephant is like a _____ because
_____.

CREATIVE WRITING: Use the following for a creative writing activity: Elephants are strong. Indian elephants can be trained to do a lot of work for people. Imagine having an elephant at your house. What kinds of work could it do for you? How would you put its strength and unusual features to good use? Write a story about keeping an elephant at your house.

SCIENCE/SOCIAL STUDIES: Gather a collection of appropriate nonfiction books and materials so that students can read and learn about the African and Indian types of elephants. Compare and contrast their likenesses and differences. Look on a world map or globe and point out their native habitats. Students can work as individuals or in small groups to write reports about their findings and share information with their classmates.

From *Daily Poetry* published by GoodYearBooks. Copyright © 1995 Carol Simpson.

GRAPHING: There are several ways you can graph the subject of elephants. One suggestion is to have the students graph their favorite type, African or Indian. Another is to have them answer "yes" or "no" to the statement, "People need elephant trunks too." Or, use a graph that explains: The neatest thing about an elephant is _____. Choices for the blank could include "its trunk," "its big ears," "its size," or "its tusks."

Name _____

I keep an elephant at my house so it can

_____

_____

_____

_____

_____

_____

_____

_____

_____

_____

_____

_____

_____

_____

From *Daily Poetry* published by GoodYearBooks. Copyright © 1995 Carol Simpson.

When You Talk to a Monkey
by
Rowena Bennett

When you talk to a monkey

He seems very wise.

He scratches his head,

And he blinks both his eyes;

But he won't say a word,

He just swings on a rail

And makes a big question mark

Out of his tail.

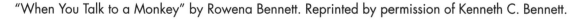

"When You Talk to a Monkey" by Rowena Bennett. Reprinted by permission of Kenneth C. Bennett.

OTHER POEMS ABOUT PRIMATES:

"The Mandrill" by Conrad Aiken (3)
"Gorilla" by Brod Bagert (20)
"Tails" by Rowena Bennett (2)

BOOKS ABOUT PRIMATES:

Koko's Kitten by Dr. Francine Patterson
Amazing Monkeys (Eyewitness Jr. series) by Scott Steedman
Extremely Weird Primates by Sarah Lovett
Arthur's Honey Bear by Lillian Hoban
Arthur's Loose Tooth by Lillian Hoban
Monkey-Monkey's Trick by Patricia McKissack
Caps for Sale by Esphyr Slobodkina
The Gorilla Did It by Barbara Shook Hazen
Little Gorilla by Ruth Bornstein
The *Curious George* series by H. A. Rey
More Spaghetti, I Say! by Rita Golden Gelman
Julius by Trygve Klingsheim
At Home in the Rain Forest by Diane Wilson

From *Daily Poetry* published by GoodYearBooks. Copyright © 1995 Carol Simpson.

EXTENDING ACTIVITIES

Primates are funny because they are so human-like. A trip to the zoo simply must include a visit to the monkey house. They make us laugh the way they climb and swing by their tails. We are in awe when we see the gorilla—the gentle giant of the rain forest. You can develop an interesting science lesson around primates by starting with a humorous poem and then extending it to include trade books and excellent nonfiction sources that are available.

LETTER/SOUND ASSOCIATIONS: This poem contains all lower-case letters except "p," "x," and "z." Several words in this poem have vowel combinations that you can introduce. Extend the learning by listing other words that contain the same combinations ("ee," "ea," and "ai"). You can work on controlled vowels ("er," "or," and "ar") in this poem. Look at the "es" and "s" suffixes as presented in the words "scratches" and "swings."

RHYMING WORDS: There are only two intended rhyming pairs in this poem. One is made with matching spelling patterns and the other by sound alone. Extend both rhyming patterns with other words that are spelled the same way. Note the placement of the rhyming words at the ends of the lines. The pattern of rhyming lines is ABCB, DEFE.

WORD FAMILIES: Two word families that can be taught and extended on charts are:

"ark" (mark, lark, bark, shark, park, spark, etc.)

"ail" (rail, tail, mail, sail, pail, fail, trail, etc.)

VOCABULARY: The text of this poem is simple and easily understood. You may want to discuss the image of the monkey, making its tail into a question mark.

SCIENCE/SOCIAL STUDIES: Gather a collection of appropriate nonfiction books that your students can use in writing group reports about various primates. Help students locate information about the size of the animals so that life-size examples can be drawn on butcher paper, cut out and then hung on the wall. You will want to have the groups present information about the animal's eating habits, its natural habitat, and any special characteristics it has. Here is an example of a class chart that could be completed as the groups present their findings. It needs to be put on very large butcher paper so that the information recorded is easily seen by everyone. Point out habitats on maps.

	SIZE	EATING HABITS	HABITAT	SPECIAL CHARACTERISTICS
MONKEY				
BABOON				
ORANGUTAN				
CHIMPANZEE				
GORILLA				

From *Daily Poetry* published by GoodYearBooks. Copyright © 1995 Carol Simpson.

MATH: Students can use the information about the sizes of primates to help sequence them in order from smallest to biggest, shortest to tallest, lightest to heaviest. If you decide to have the students make life-sized drawings of their primates, they will need to be able to do measuring. A simple way to do this activity is to cut a large supply of "feet" out of construction paper. Be sure that they are 12" long. If an animal is 6' tall a student will place six of the measuring feet end to end to show that animal's height. The gorilla can have an arm span of 9'. To measure it, place nine "feet" end to end and they will know how far a gorilla can reach.

EXTEND WITH A BOOK: The book *Caps For Sale* by Esphyr Slobodkina is a humorous account of monkeys who manage to steal a pile of caps from a vendor and will not give them back. The monkeys in the story do not talk. They are presented as very natural and curious. Monkeys are often presented in naughty but humorous ways in trade books. Discuss the idea of getting into "monkey business." What does it mean? Is it bad? Is it good? Do you get into monkey business sometimes? *Koko's Kitten* by Dr. Francine Patterson offers an excellent true story, complete with photographs, about a gorilla and his pet kitty. The gorilla learns to communicate with a human. It is a fascinating story to share with young readers.

MYSTERY WORD: When you write the poem of the week on a chart, you may want to omit the word "monkey" from the title and the first line. Read the poem, leaving out the word, and see if your students can predict that the missing word is "monkey." What clues helped the students determine the mystery word? Are there other words that might fit in the poem instead?

CREATIVE WRITING: Discuss the following for creative writing: We think of monkeys as being funny and cute but naughty. If one would get loose in your house, you would not be very happy about the monkey business it would get into. Write a story about a monkey getting loose in your house and what happens. How do you capture the monkey? Where does it really belong? How did it get into your house in the first place?

Name_____

A monkey got loose in my house and

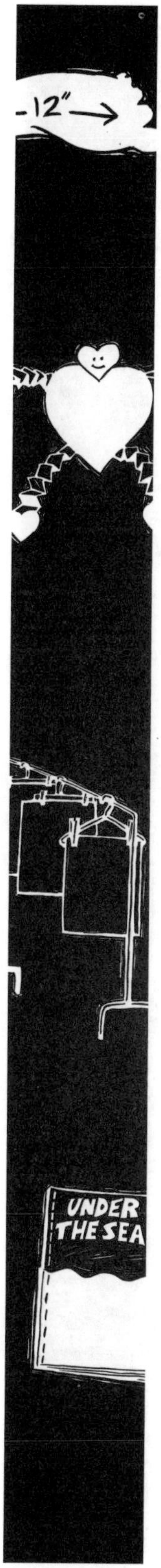

_____

_____

_____

_____

_____

_____

_____

_____

_____

_____

_____

_____

_____

_____

If You Should Meet
A
Crocodile
Anonymous

If you should meet a Crocodile

Don't take a stick and poke him;

Ignore the welcome in his smile,

Be careful not to stroke him.

For as he sleeps upon the Nile,

He thinner gets and thinner;

And whene'er you meet a Crocodile

He's ready for his dinner.

From *Daily Poetry* published by GoodYearBooks. Copyright © 1995 Carol Simpson.

OTHER POEMS ABOUT REPTILES AND AMPHIBIANS:

"Garden Snake" by Muriel L. Sonne (1)
"Summer" by Caryl M. Kerber (1)
"The Little Turtle" by Vachel Lindsay (2, 14)
"The Lizard" by John Gardner (3, 6)
"The Crocodile" by Lewis Carroll (3, 6, 13)
"The Frog" by Hilaire Belloc (3, 13)
"The Alligator" by Mary Macdonald (3)
"The Crocodile's Toothache" by Shel Silverstein (21)
"Alligators Are Unfriendly" by Jack Prelutsky (22)

BOOKS ABOUT REPTILES AND AMPHIBIANS:

The Smallest Turtle by Lynley Dodd
Amazing Frogs and Toads (Eyewitness Jr. series) by Barry Clarke
My World: Different Kinds of Snakes by Donna Bailey
My World: Frogs and Toads by Christine Butterworth
My World: Alligators and Crocodiles by Donna Bailey & others
Frogs, Toads, Lizards, and Salamanders by Nancy W. Parker
The Frog Alphabet Book by Jerry Pallotta
Hide and Snake by Keith Baker
Extremely Weird Reptiles by Sarah Lovett
Extremely Weird Frogs by Sarah Lovett
Snakes and Other Reptiles by Steven Lindblom
An Alligator Named Alligator by Lois Grambling
The Enormous Crocodile by Roald Dahl
Jerome the Baby-Sitter by Eileen Christelow
Elizabeth and Larry by Marilyn Sadler
The *Lyle Crocodile* series by Bernard Waber
The *Frog and Toad* series by Arnold Lobel
Mama Don't Allow by Thacher Hurd
Tuesday by David Weisner
Crictor by Tomi Ungerer

EXTENDING ACTIVITIES

Here is yet another opportunity to present a factual unit about two animal groups that fascinate children. You will want to choose your trade books carefully so as to include humorous stories as well as nonfiction material that presents new information to your classroom.

LETTER/SOUND ASSOCIATIONS: There are several words that begin with blends featuring the letter "s" ("st," "sm," "str," "sl"), as well as the "sh" sound. You can teach the "ck" and "ke" patterns: -ck follows a short vowel, "ke" follows a long vowel). You can teach long "a," "e," "i," and "o" sounds in words in this poem. The same short vowels are also included. Find and name the appropriate words with short and long vowels and compare their spelling patterns.

RHYMING WORDS: This ABABCDCD pattern poem has special ways to make the rhyming pairs. The second and fourth lines require two-word phrases to sound like rhyming pairs ("poke him" and "stroke him"). Take note of the placement of the rhymes at the ends of lines of print.

WORD FAMILIES: Two word families that you might teach and present on charts are:

"-ile" (smile, mile, while, pile, tile, etc.)
"-oke" (poke, stroke, joke, smoke, choke, etc.)

From *Daily Poetry* published by GoodYearBooks. Copyright © 1995 Carol Simpson.

VOCABULARY: Several contractions can be pointed out. The word "whene'er" is an unusual contraction. See if students can determine which two words were put together and what letter was left out. Change contractions into the two words that were put together to make one, and see what happens to the rhythm of the poem when read as two words. Locate the Nile on a world map and point out that it is the name of an important river.

EXTEND WITH A BOOK: There are several *Frog and Toad* books by Arnold Lobel. Each one contains a collection of stories. Ask pairs of students to work together as they read a story from a *Frog and Toad* book and share the plot with the class. Compare and contrast the two characters in the stories that are presented. Relate the friendship of the two characters to human friendships that exist within the classroom. Discuss the human-like characteristics that make Frog and Toad good friends to have.

SCIENCE/SOCIAL STUDIES: Groups of students can use nonfiction sources to read about different reptiles and amphibians. Have them present information to their classmates about their animal's habitat, eating habits, size, and special characteristics. Be prepared with a globe or world map so that the natural habitats of the animals can be located. You may want to prepare another chart that is similar to the one suggested in the primates lesson in order to record important information uncovered in research.

CREATIVE WRITING: Discuss the following for creative writing: Most people would agree that reptiles and amphibians are not pretty animals. They have attributes that make them ugly, even frightening to many people. What could a frog do to become more attractive to people? Write a story about it.

Name_____

If a frog wants to be pretty it will have to

_____
_____
_____
_____
_____
_____
_____
_____
_____
_____
_____
_____
_____
_____
_____

Cute Pig
by
Ruby Bailey and
Carol Simpson

A little pig is very cute

With curly tail and turned up snoot,

Floppy ears and pudgy face,

A mud hole is his favorite place.

If only he'd stay clean he'd be

The perfect pet to play with me.

They say he's smart as any dog.

Too bad he turns into a hog.

OTHER POEMS ABOUT PIGS:

"A Pig Tale" by James Reeves (2, 14)
"The Pig" by Roland Young (3)
"A Pig Is Never Blamed" by Babette Deutsch (3)
"I Had a Little Pig" by Anonymous (3)
"As I looked Out" by Anonymous (13)
"Whose Little Pigs?" by Anonymous (13)
"There Was a Pig" by Lewis Carroll (13)

BOOKS ABOUT PIGS:

Pigs Aplenty, Pigs Galore by David McPhail
The Piggest Show on Earth by Arlene Dubanevich
Pigs in Hiding by Arlene Dubanevich
Pig William by Arlene Dubanevich
The Piggy in the Puddle by Charlotte Pomerantz
Small Pig by Arnold Lobel
Piggybook by Anthony Browne
Wriggles, the Little Wishing Pig by Pauline Watson
Oh, What a Mess by Marilyn Sapienza
If I Had a Pig by Mick Inkpen
The *Pig Pig* series by David McPhail
Tales of Oliver Pig by Jean Van Leeuwen
Oliver, Amanda, and Grandmother Pig by Jean Van Leeuwen
Pigs by Robert Munsch
The Pig Who Saved the Day by Thomas Crawford
Three Little Pigs by James Marshall
The True Story of The Three Pigs by Jon Scieszka
Charlotte's Web by E. B. White
Perfect the Pig by Susan Jeschke

From *Daily Poetry* published by GoodYearBooks. Copyright © 1995 Carol Simpson.

EXTENDING ACTIVITIES

Here is a lesson that doesn't require extensive research about an animal group, although it is possible to study different kinds of pigs. This poem and accompanying materials are presented simply as a fun lesson. Children might discover that pigs are not necessarily the smelly animals they think they are.

LETTER/SOUND ASSOCIATIONS: Several words in this poem present two sounds of the letter "y" as it ends a word with one or two syllables. The short and long "u" sounds can both be presented, as well as the "ur" controlled vowel sound. The soft "c" (place) and hard "c" (clean) are both included in the poem. Find all the "c's" in the poem and identify the sounds they make.

RHYMING WORDS: This poem utilizes the pattern of having pairs of adjacent lines rhyme. All rhyming pairs have like spelling patterns except for "cute" and "snoot." When the poem is read aloud, be sure to allow students to chant the second word of a rhyming pair.

WORD FAMILIES: Two word families you might introduce and extend are:

"art" (smart, art, part, dart, cart, mart, chart, etc.)
"ad" (bad, sad, mad, dad, glad, fad, had, pad, etc.)

VOCABULARY: The word "snoot" is used to suggest what part of the pig's body? What is a pudgy face? There are many descriptive words in the poem. Find and underline all words and phrases that tell something about a pig. Why is it a negative notion that the pig "turns into a hog"? There are two contractions that can be located and formed into two words. Find the compound word and use a slash line (/) to separate the word into two words.

SHOW AND TELL: If you live near a rural area, see if you can get someone to bring a baby pig to your class. It would be fun for the children to see a baby pig in person, to get to touch it and hear it squeal. You may want to make two lists of pig characteristics—one before the pig visits, and one after the pig has come to class. See if there are any changes and corrections to make.

GRAPHING: The poem of the week suggests that a pig would be a good pet. Graph that idea by having the students color in a space or write their names to respond to the sentence: "I'd like a pig for a pet."

CREATIVE WRITING: Assign the following for creative writing: Pigs are really smart animals. If you had a pig for a pet, you could teach it new tricks. Write a story about just how smart your pet pig is.

COMPARE/CONTRAST TRADE BOOKS: Read a typical version of the story of *"The Three Little Pigs."* Then share Jon Scieszka's *The True Story of the Three Pigs.* Compare and contrast the two versions. Which one are your students more inclined to believe? You may be surprised at the terrific class discussions and arguments you will get into when students are encouraged to give reasons for believing the wolf's version over the traditional story and why.

From *Daily Poetry* published by GoodYearBooks. Copyright © 1995 Carol Simpson.

ILLUSTRATE A STORY: E. B. White's *Charlotte's Web* is a favorite chapter book among many children. Share the book, one or two chapters a day, until the book is finished. Each day, ask one or two children to draw pictures that show what happened in the story that day. Let students dictate sentences that describe the pictures. Put all of the pictures together into a book and let students take it home to share with their families.

Name _____

My pet pig is so smart_____

_____

_____

_____

_____

_____

_____

_____

_____

_____

_____

_____

_____

_____

The Brave Mouse
by
Irene Rawnsley

Annabel,

Annabel,

Come and see here;

A mouse is asleep

In tabby cat's ear!

He climbed up her tail

As she lay in a heap;

Ran over her body

Then fell fast asleep.

I wonder

I wonder

For brown mouse's sake

If he or if tabby

Will be first awake?

"The Brave Mouse" by Irene Rawnsley. Copyright © 1990 by Irene Rawnsley.
Reprinted by permission of Oxford University Press, Oxford, England.

OTHER POEMS ABOUT MICE:

"Mice" by Rose Fyleman (2, 3, 14)
"My Name is Supermouse" by John Kitching (7)
"A Mouse in Her Room" by Anonymous (13)
"Who Lived in a Shoe?" by Beatrix Potter (2)
"Nine Mice" by Jack Prelutsky (22)
"Boing! Boing! Squeak!" by Jack Prelutsky (22)

BOOKS ABOUT MICE:

Mouse Poems compiled by John Foster
Seven Blind Mice by Ed Young
Tomato Soup by Thacher Hurd
Frederick by Leo Lionni
Mrs. Brice's Mice by Syd Hoff
The *Anatole* series by Eve Titus
Ralph S. Mouse by Beverly Cleary
Runaway Mouse by Beverly Cleary
The Mouse and the Motorcycle by Beverly Cleary
Alexander and the Wind-Up Mouse by Leo Lionni
Noisy Nora by Rosemary Wells
Do You Want to Be My Friend? by Eric Carle
Whose Mouse Are You? by Robert Kraus
Nosey Mrs. Rat by Allen Jeffrey
Pet of the Met by Don Freeman
Sheila Rae, the Brave by Kevin Henkes
If You Give a Mouse a Cookie by Laura Numeroff
Mouse Around by Pat Schories
Rosie's Mouse by Gina & Mercer Mayer
I Love You, Mouse by John Graham
Cats and Mice by Rita Golden Gelman
The City Mouse and the Country Mouse by Aesop
The Lion and the Mouse by Aesop
Little Ego by Frank Gilroy
Pearl's Pirates by Frank Asch

From *Daily Poetry* published by GoodYearBooks. Copyright © 1995 Carol Simpson.

EXTENDING ACTIVITIES

Mice are tiny, but they frighten a lot of people. The poems and trade books that are listed with this lesson present mice in a more favorable light. Mice are not something to be afraid of. They are really shy and would prefer to hide and stay away from people. Have fun with this lesson as you write stories and read humorous poems and trade books.

LETTER/SOUND ASSOCIATIONS: There are two spellings of the "ou" and "ow" sound (as in "mouse" and "brown") in this poem. Locate all long or short vowels in the poem and identify their sounds. Which words follow the vowel rules? Which ones do not? Find a word with a silent letter ("climbed").

RHYMING WORDS: Two verses in this poem have five lines instead of four. The first two lines of these verses are identical. Find the rhyming words at the ends of the appropriate lines and underline them. Note the different spelling patterns and write more words that fit each of these patterns.

WORD FAMILIES: Be prepared with chart paper for doing the following two suggested word families:

"an" (ran, can, man, plan, van, than, fan, etc.)
"ee" (see, tree, free, agree, bee, etc.)

VOCABULARY: The "'s" possessive is presented in this poem ("cat's," "mouse's"). Explain the "ed" suffix in the word climbed. Here is an opportunity to explore the past tense in other forms: come/came, see/saw, is/was, run/ran, fall/fell. There are several prepositional phrases that tell the places where the mouse went. Find and underline or circle these phrases.

WRITING PREPOSITIONS: Everyone in class can contribute a page of "The Mouse's Adventure," a class book, by completing the following sentence with a prepositional phrase and adding an appropriate illustration.

The mouse went _____

EXTEND WITH A BOOK: Read a version of Aesop's *The City Mouse and the Country Mouse.* Compare and contrast the two mice in the story. Each mouse thinks that his home is best. Ask the students the following: If you were one of the characters, which one would you want to be? Would you want to have good food to eat but have to be on the lookout for a cat all of the time? Or, would you settle for seeds and have the freedom of the field?

GRAPHING: There are many mice in stories. Brainstorm a list of mice. Students then will draw a picture and label each mouse on the graph. Choices may be as varied as Mickey Mouse, the City Mouse, the Country Mouse, Leo Lionni's Frederick, or Beverly Cleary's Ralph S. Mouse. The number of graph lines you make will depend upon how many different mice are represented. Have each student write his or her name by his or her favorite mouse.

CREATIVE WRITING: Have students think about and write on the following: What might happen if mice were not so small? How would cats feel if mice were their size? Would they still chase them? Would they try hard to get along with one another? Write a story about a cat and a mouse that are the same size.

Name _____

I know a mouse and a cat that are the same size, and they like to

_____

_____

_____

_____

_____

_____

_____

_____

_____

_____

_____

_____

_____

Baby Chick
by
Aileen Fisher

Peck

peck

peck

on the warm brown egg.

OUT comes a neck.

OUT comes a leg.

How

does

a chick

who's not been about,

discover the trick

of how to get out?

OTHER POEMS ABOUT FEATHERED FRIENDS:

"The Canary" by Ogden Nash (3)
"The Blackbird" by Humbert Wolfe (3)
"Sea Gull" by Elizabeth Coatsworth (3)
"The Hen" by Lord Alfred Douglas (3)
"The Vulture" by Hilaire Belloc (3)
"The Eagle" by Alfred Lord Tennyson (3)
"They've All Gone South" by Mary Britton Miller (3)
"Pigeons" by Lilian Moore (3)
"Wild Geese" by Sandra Liatsos (4)
"The Duck" by Ogden Nash (6, 14)
"Sparrow" by Kaye Starbird (6)
"The Red Hen" by James S. Tippett (6)
"I Had a Little Hen" by Anonymous (13)
"A Robin" by Aileen Fisher (15)
"The Toucan" by Shel Silverstein (21)

BOOKS ABOUT FEATHERED FRIENDS:

The Egg (First Discovery Series) by Gillimard Jeunesse and others
The Bird Alphabet Book by Jerry Pallotta
Chickens Aren't the Only Ones by Ruth Heller
Hattie and the Fox by Mem Fox
The Mountain That Loved a Bird by Alice McLerran
Rosie's Walk by Pat Hutchins
Have You Seen My Duckling? by Nancy Tafuri
Rooster's Off to See the World by Eric Carle
Petunia by Roger Duvoisin
Make Way for Ducklings by Robert McCloskey
Backyard Birds by Jonathan Pine
Buck Buck the Chicken by Amy Erlich
The Golden Goose by Brothers Grimm
Chicken Little by Steven Kellogg
The Case of the Elevator Duck by Polly Berends

EXTENDING ACTIVITIES

Feathered friends come in all sizes and colors. All birds come from eggs. Most can fly. Indeed, birds remind us of a wish we all have had at one time or another: to be able to fly, to soar high above the earth. We see the V-formation of the flocks of geese as they fly south for the winter. Birds also can be found in everyone's backyard. They are fun to watch and feed. Everyone knows about feathered friends.

LETTER/SOUND ASSOCIATIONS: Many words in the poem have the "ou" or "ow" sound. Find those words, underline them, and take note of the two ways to spell that sound. There are many short "e" words to locate. Look closely at the CVC or CVCC pattern of some of them.

RHYMING WORDS: The rhyming words in this poem are not found at the end of every line of print because of the way the first three lines of each verse are spaced—one or two words to a line. Which of the words is intended as a rhyme? Say the poem aloud. When students hear a rhyme, they need to raise their hands and tell what two words sound the same. Then the words can be located and underlined in the poem. Other words with the same spelling patterns also can be introduced.

WORD FAMILIES: Two families that can be taught along with this poem are:

"own" (brown, town, down, frown, clown, crown, etc.)
"ick" (chick, pick, trick, sick, lick, thick, Rick, stick, etc.)

VOCABULARY: Ask the students to find a word that tells what scientists do ("discover"). Find two words that name body parts ("neck," "leg"). Find words that describe the egg ("warm," "brown"). Can eggs be found in other colors? Are chicks the only things that come out of an egg? Why does this poem end with a question mark?

DRAMATIZATION: The words of this poem suggest actions that can be performed as the poem is read aloud. Start small, like a ball, then "peck" with fingers and begin to climb out of the egg, a neck, a leg. Soon you are a whole chick. Why do you think the poet wrote the word "OUT" in all capital letters in two places in the poem?

CLASS WISH BOOK: Each member of the class can contribute a page of a class wish book that tells about something a feathered friend can do that we cannot do.

I wish I could _____ like a _____.

Illustrations should be drawn for each page. Combine the pages and bind them together. Let students take home the class book to share.

EXTEND WITH A BOOK: The Pat Hutchins story *Rosie's Walk* is written from the hen's perspective. There is another character in the story. Try to get student input as you write FOX'S WALK. You can use many sound words such as CRASH ! or POOF! Use sticky notes on the pages of the book as you write the story the children dictate. They will delight in reading their new story.

GRAPHING: Think of attributes of our feathered friends. Some examples might be that they can fly (most can), they lay eggs, they have feathers, or they have a beak. Graph the following by having the students color or write their names in the appropriate space for their responses.

I THINK FEATHERED FRIENDS ARE SPECIAL BECAUSE THEY:							
FLY							
HAVE FEATHERS							
LAY EGGS							
HAVE BEAKS							

CREATIVE WRITING: Assign the following for creative writing: Feathered friends come from eggs. Pretend that you found an egg and you do not know what will hatch out of it. Write a story that describes what you hope will appear when the egg cracks open. Ruth Heller's book *Chickens Aren't the Only Ones* presents information about numerous things that hatch from eggs. It may be good to read this book before writing your egg story.

From *Daily Poetry* published by GoodYearBooks. Copyright © 1995 Carol Simpson.

Name_____

I found an egg. It's going to hatch! I hope that

_____

_____

_____

_____

_____

_____

_____

_____

_____

_____

_____

_____

_____

_____

_____

_____

MOTHER NATURE

The six poems in this unit deal with the world outdoors, the world just beyond the backdoor where we can explore small creatures and how they move, animal homes, plants, and the weather. We will also examine modes of travel, by humans as well as by critters. This unit will help students become more aware of the world just outside their door and will encourage them to try to be more careful when entering Mother Nature's domain.

It is possible to use each of the six lessons at separate times during the school year. "Creepy Crawlies" can be done either in the fall when the insects and spiders are plentiful and caterpillars are going to make their cocoons, or in the spring when they begin to appear after the long winter. It may be effective to study "Weather" when the seasonal changes are very obvious in the fall, or when the snow is falling, or when spring arrives and it becomes warm, rainy and stormy. The theme of "Locomotion" may be useful (and in some cases acted out) during the long days of winter when it is too cold to be outside. "Seeds" is always a good topic of study in the spring when it it time to plant them.

Flexibility is the key here. The teacher can decide when and how it is most appropriate to use the poems in this unit.

From *Daily Poetry* published by GoodYearBooks. Copyright © 1995 Carol Simpson.

Snail
by
John Drinkwater

Snail upon the wall,

Have you got at all

Anything to tell

About your shell?

Only this, my child—

When the wind is wild,

Or when the sun is hot,

It's all I've got.

OTHER POEMS ABOUT THE GARDEN:

"Our Garden's Flower Parade" by Leland B. Jacobs (1)
"Dandelions" by Hazel Cederborg (1)
"Mud" by Polly Chase Boyden (3)
"The Muddy Puddle" by Dennis Lee (3)
"Busy" by Phyllis Halloran (6)
"The Flying Squirrel" by John Gardner (6)
"The Bird's Nest" by John Drinkwater (6)
"I Have to Have It" by Dorothy Aldis (7)
"The Digging Song" by Wes Magee (7)
"Our Pond" by Richard Edwards (8)
"The Tree in Season" by Robert Fisher (8)
"The Gardener" by Robert Louis Stevenson (9)
"Nest Eggs" by Robert Louis Stevenson (9)
"The Camping Spot" by Jane Baskwill (12)
"Our Tree" by Marchette Chute (14)
"Trees" by Harry Behn (15)

BOOKS ABOUT THE GARDEN:

First Nature Watch: The Hare by Ruth Hurlimann
Trees by Harry Behn
The Garden Walked Away by Elva Robinson
Backyard Insects by Millicent E. Selsam
Amazing Spiders by Alexandra Parsons
The Reason for a Flower by Ruth Heller
The Amazing World of Night Creatures by Janet Craig
The Amazing World of Spiders by Janet Craig
Amelia Bedelia Goes Camping by Peggy Parish
Demi's Secret Garden by Demi
In the Tall, Tall Grass by Denise Fleming
In a Small, Small Pond by Denise Fleming
Cactus Hotel by Brenda Z. Guiberson
Always Room for One More by Sorche Nic Leodhas
The Longest Journey in the World by William Barrett Morris

EXTENDING ACTIVITIES

The theme of this lesson is "Out in the Garden," but that does not necessarily mean that the subject is "gardening." Flowers, bugs, snails, trees, even mud puddles, can be discussed with this topic. Children will be asked to talk about things they know well, the natural phenomena they have experienced when they have played outside.

LETTER/SOUND ASSOCIATIONS: If you have not yet worked on ending sounds, you might wish to work on words that end with "l" and "ll." Compare the single and double consonant sounds. Is there a difference? Do you hear both of the letters in words such as "wall" or "all"? Or do two consonants make only one sound? What other combinations of double consonants are common? ("ss," "tt," "nn," "gg," "dd")—You may also want to discuss the "ck" combination as a single sound with two different consonants.

RHYMING WORDS: Find and underline the pairs of rhyming words. Note the AABB rhyming pattern of the two verses. In this poem, all rhyming pairs are spelled with similar word families. Note also the placement of rhyming words at the ends of the lines of print.

WORD FAMILIES: Two suggested rhyming families to put on charts are:

"ild" (child, wild, mild, etc.)

"un" (sun, run, fun, gun, spun, shun, etc.)

From *Daily Poetry* published by GoodYearBooks. Copyright © 1995 Carol Simpson.

VOCABULARY: There are contraction words to locate and turn into two words. There are also compound words to mark with a slash (/) to separate the two words. Most of the words in this poem consist of a single syllable. Can your students find the words with two or more syllables and underline them? Ask students what the message in the poem might be. What is meant by the words "It's all I've got"?

SCIENCE/SOCIAL STUDIES: Brainstorm a list of things you might find in your backyard. Sort them into living and nonliving things. Sort living things into plants and animals. Ask students to imagine that they lived in a different environment (a desert, the mountains, a rain forest, or the beach). Locate the new environment on a globe or map. What different things would they find in their new backyards?

HELPING YOUR ANIMAL FRIENDS: Have each student make a feeder so they can feed and observe the birds, squirrels, rabbits, raccoons, etc., that frequent their backyards. Ask them to record their observations and share them with classmates.

MAKE A BOOK: Make a pop-up class or group book with each child contributing a page about a backyard animal. They will need to write a short description of the animal and make a pop-up figure of it to attach to the center seam of the page.

EXTEND WITH A BOOK: Share the story of *The Longest Journey in the World* by William Barrett Morris. The story describes the garden as it is seen by a tiny caterpillar. Ask children to imagine the world as it might be seen from a different perspective.

CREATIVE WRITING: Have students write a story about a snail's journey across their own backyard. What hazards would it find? How long might it take?

From *Daily Poetry* published by GoodYearBooks. Copyright © 1995 Carol Simpson.

Name _____

I am a snail on a journey. I need to get to the other side of the backyard but it won't be easy.

_____

_____

_____

_____

_____

_____

_____

_____

_____

_____

_____

_____

_____

_____

_____

_____

Homes Everywhere
by
Carol Simpson

Living creatures need a home,

A place to call their own.

A den, a nest, a web, a barn,

Or even under a stone.

A shell, a box, a hole in a tree,

A home can be anywhere.

Remember when you're out exploring

To treat nature's homes with care.

OTHER POEMS ABOUT HOMES:

"A House for One" by Laura Arlon (1)
"Snail" by John Drinkwater (2, 6, 14)
"Tree House" by Shel Silverstein (2)
"Houses" by Mary Britton Miller (2, 14)
"Our House" by Dorothy Brown Thompson (3)
"A House" by Charlotte Zolotow (4)
"Under Stepping Stones" by Brod Bagert (20)
"Tree House" by Shel Silverstein (21)

BOOKS ABOUT HOMES:

A House Is a House for Me by Mary Ann Hoberman
At Home in the Rain Forest by Diane Willow
People by Peter Spier
The Napping House by Audrey Wood
Good-Bye House by Frank Asch
Home for a Dinosaur by Eileen Curran
Searchin' Safari by Jeff O'Hare
This Is the Place for Me by Joanna Cole
The Big Orange Splot by Daniel Pinkwater
Building a House by Byron Barton
Too Much Noise by Ann McGovern
A Very Special House by Ruth Krauss
The Little House by Virginia Lee Burton
Houses of Hide and Earth by Bonnie Shemie
Houses of Bark by Bonnie Shemie
Houses of Snow, Skin and Bones by Bonnie Shemie
And So They Build by Bert Kitchen
What's in the Cave? by Peter Seymour

EXTENDING ACTIVITIES

This lesson introduces homes of all kinds. People homes, animal homes, even some homes you never thought about before. The poem and its related activities will help students become more aware of all the homes around them when they step outside the door.

LETTER/SOUND ASSOCIATIONS: Locate and underline the letter "c" each time it appears in the poem. Determine whether the letter makes a hard "k" sound or soft "s" sound. Find all the words that have a long vowel sound and see if you can determine which long vowel rule applies in each situation. Many words have consonant blends. Find those blends, underline or circle them, and try to name other words that begin or end with the same sound. Locate the words that contain the letter "x" and say the words aloud. What two consonants blend together to make that letter sound ("ks")? Look in a dictionary to find words that begin with "x." You will not find many. Then check how many pages of words you find that begin with "b" or "s." You will find many more.

RHYMING WORDS: The rhyming pattern is ABCBDEFE. Find the rhyming pairs and underline them in like colors. Note the spelling pattern differences. List other words that contain those same spelling patterns. Note the placement of rhyming words at the ends of some of the lines of print.

From *Daily Poetry* published by GoodYearBooks. Copyright © 1995 Carol Simpson.

WORD FAMILIES: Many word families could be presented by using the words in this poem. Try the following:

"eat" (treat, seat, meat, beat, heat, wheat, etc.)

"ace" (place, race, lace, space, face, grace, etc.)

VOCABULARY: Locate and underline or circle all words that name places which might be a home for one of nature's creatures. Find prepositional phrases in the poem. The apostrophe is used in two different ways in the poem. Locate the apostrophes and tell which one is used to show ownership and which one denotes a contraction word. Note the commas in a series as presented in the third and fifth lines of the poem.

NATURE WALK: Take a walk near your school. Look for animal homes. Be sure to look "under a stone" and in "a hole in a tree" to find signs of something living there. Write a class experience story about the nature walk.

SOCIAL STUDIES: Construct a neighborhood model on a table top. Using milk cartons and small boxes, students can make their homes. Make streets and sidewalks out of construction paper, trees and bushes out of clay or cotton balls and sticks. Each student can locate his or her home on the "map" and describe his or her daily journey to and from school.

EXTEND WITH A BOOK: Read *A House Is a House for Me* by Mary Ann Hoberman. This book suggests all kinds of homes that one usually does not think about. Each student can contribute a page to a class collection about homes by completing the following sentence.

A _____ is a house for a _____.

CREATIVE WRITING: Brainstorm a list of homes in nature. Discuss the possibility of trading places with one of the animals and have the students write on the following: If you could trade places, in which new home would you want to live? Describe your life in the treetops, in the river, or on a mountain cliff. What animal are you? How did you choose your home? Is it safe? Who are your enemies and how are you protected from them?

Name_____

I'm trading places with a _____

so I can live _____

Poetry File

Caterpillars
by
Brod Bagert

They came like dew drops overnight

Eating every plant in sight,

Those nasty worms with legs that crawl

So creepy up the garden wall,

Green prickly fuzz to hurt and sting

Each unsuspecting living thing.

How I hate them! Oh, you know

I'd love to squish them with my toe.

But then I see past their disguise,

Someday they'll all be butterflies.

From *Daily Poetry* published by GoodYearBooks. Copyright © 1995 Carol Simpson.

OTHER POEMS ABOUT CREEPY CRAWLY THINGS:

"The Insects' World" by Ethel Jacobson (1)

"The Ants' Picnic" by Carol Quinn (1)

"Cricket Song" by Elsie M. Strachan (1)

"Trusting Butterfly" by Claire Boiko (1)

"Fireflies" by Aileen Fisher (1)

"Firefly" by Elizabeth Maddox Roberts (2, 6, 14)

"The Caterpillar" by Christina Rossetti (2, 3, 5, 14)

"Hey, Bug!" by Lilian Moore (3)

"Hurt No Living Thing" by Christina Rossetti (3)

"The Bug" by Marjorie Barrows (3)

"The Tickle Rhyme" by Ian Serraillier (5)

"Every Insect" by Dorothy Aldis (6)

"Crickets" by Harry Behn (6)

"Bee! I'm Expecting You" by Emily Dickinson (6)

BOOKS ABOUT CREEPY CRAWLY THINGS:

The Garden Walked Away by Elva Robinson

The Ladybug (First Discovery Series) by Gallimard Jeunesse and others

Backyard Insects by Millicent E. Selsam

Old Black Fly by Jim Aylesworth

The Itsy Bitsy Spider by Iza Trapani

Two Bad Ants by Chris Van Allsburg

The Icky Bug Alphabet Book by Jerry Pallotta

Golly Gump Swallowed a Fly by Joanna Cole

Buzz Buzz Buzz by Byron Barton

The Very Quiet Cricket by Eric Carle

The Grouchy Ladybug by Eric Carle

The Very Hungry Caterpillar by Eric Carle

The Very Busy Spider by Eric Carle

Anansi the Spider by Gerald McDermott

Anansi and the Moss Covered Rock by Eric Kimmel

EXTENDING ACTIVITIES

"Creepy Crawlies" can be found everywhere. Some children delight in observing them. Others think they are awful creatures. Perhaps a closer look at some of nature's creepy crawlies will help the squeamish appreciate their presence. There are many good poems and books about them. This lesson provides you with an opportunity (or an excuse, if you will) to bring in a caterpillar and watch it as it transforms into a beautiful butterfly or moth.

LETTER/SOUND ASSOCIATIONS: Underline the letter "a" whenever you find it, and then identify the sound it makes. You will find words with long a, short "a," "aw," "ar," "all," and even silent "a." What other word sounds as though it has the letter "a" in it, but does not? (they) Other controlled vowels ("er," "or," "ur," "ir") can also be identified and underlined. If you are still going on a letter search, you will find all but the letters "j" and "x" in this poem. You can work on double consonants in the words "fuzz," "wall," "all," and "butterflies." You can also present the "ck" as being similar to a double consonant in the word "prickly."

RHYMING WORDS: All rhyming pairs in the poem have two different spelling patterns, with the exception of "overnight/sight." It is important to point out the differences in the others. Note, also, the placement of rhyming words at the ends of the lines of print. The AABBCCDDEE pattern of rhyme can be identified.

From *Daily Poetry* published by GoodYearBooks. Copyright © 1995 Carol Simpson.

WORD FAMILIES: Numerous word families are present in this poem. It therefore may be a good time to try a word family spinner. This is similar to an alphabet spinner, described in "How to Use This Book" (page 1), but it has common word families in place of letters of the alphabet. The families that are suggested for charting along with this lesson are:

"ant" (plant, grant, pant, ant, chant, slant, etc.)

"ew" (dew, new, knew, few, chew, crew, drew, etc.)

VOCABULARY: You may want to introduce words such as "prickly," "disguise," and "unsuspecting" before reading the poem. What are dew drops? How does the poet feel about caterpillars at the beginning of the poem? Does his attitude change by the end? Find another word that could replace "squish" and write it on a sticky note. Find all the negative descriptive words used: words such as "nasty," "creepy," "prickly," "to hurt and sting." Can you change these words so that the poem is not so negative about caterpillars?

EXTEND WITH A BOOK: *Anansi and the Moss Covered Rock* by Eric Kimmel is a tale about a spider who tries to trick his jungle neighbors out of their food. Some students may be familiar with *Anansi the Spider* by Gerald McDermott, an Ashanti tale about a spider with special powers. Compare and contrast the two stories. Ask the students: Which one is your favorite story? Why?

GRAPHING: Graph the following sentence:

I LIKE CREEPY CRAWLIES !

YES, I DO							
NO, I DON'T							

SCIENCE: Collect live creepy crawlies and keep them in a habitat. Whether it be a store-bought bug box or something made from scratch, a habitat is good for observing a caterpillar as it makes its transformation, a cricket as it rubs its legs together, a walking stick, or a spider as it makes a web. Students may catch a variety of bugs to observe. Be sure to gather a good collection of nonfiction materials that students can read to learn more about the creepy crawly things they are observing.

REWRITE A FAMILIAR STORY: Eric Carle's story *The Very Hungry Caterpillar* is familiar to everyone. Try writing a new story using the same pattern: a creature eating some kind of food all the days of the week and in increasing numbers. Your students' creature may or may not take on a new appearance after it matures into an adult of its species. Perhaps it just gets a terrible stomachache in the end !

OUTDOOR ART PROJECT: Share the story of *Old Black Fly* by Jim Aylesworth. As a followup, IF the weather cooperates—that is, if there is no wind and the temperature is warm enough to allow you to go outside—you might try a fun but messy painting project. Dip flyswatters in red, yellow, blue, and other colors of paint and then SPLAT them on a large piece of drawing paper. Make sure you have enough flyswatters so that they do not need to be used in more than one paint tin because the colors will get mixed together. Also, be sure that those awaiting a turn sit far away from the splatting flyswatters or they will get covered with paint. When the paintings have dried, you can glue a black construction paper fly on the picture. This project is guaranteed to be a very memorable one!

CREATIVE WRITING: Butterflies are among the most colorful of nature's wonders. It might be nice to be a butterfly for a day or a season and be free to wander here and there. Ask your students: What would you do if you could be a butterfly? Where would you go? What might you see? How would you keep from being caught in a butterfly net? Have them write a story about their adventures as a butterfly.

Name _____

I am a butterfly and I can _____

_____

_____

_____

_____

_____

_____

_____

_____

_____

_____

_____

_____

From *Daily Poetry* published by GoodYearBooks. Copyright © 1995 Carol Simpson.

Leap and Dance
Anonymous

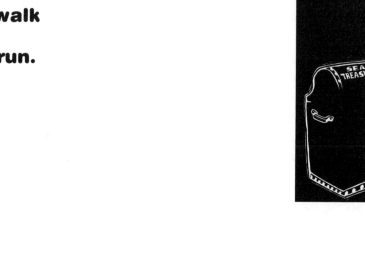

The lion walks on padded paws,

The squirrel leaps from limb to limb,

While flies can crawl straight up a wall,

And seals can dive and swim.

The worm, it wiggles all around,

The monkey swings by its tail,

And birds may hop upon the ground,

Or spread their wings and sail.

But boys and girls have much more fun;

They leap and dance

And walk

And run.

OTHER POEMS ABOUT LOCOMOTION:

"Roller Skating" by Irene B. Crofoot (1)

"Away We Go" by Eleanor Dennis (1)

"Jumping Rope" by Lee Blair (1)

"Merry-Go-Round" by Margaret Hillert (1)

"The Ferris Wheel" by Josephine Van Dolzen Pease (1)

"Preferred Vehicles" by Leland B. Jacobs (1)

"Kangaroo Ride" by Elaine V. Emans (1)

"Jump or Jiggle" by Evelyn Beyer (1)

"On Our Way" by Eve Mirriam (2, 5, 14)

"The Swing" by Robert Louis Stevenson (2, 4, 9, 14)

"Sing a Song of Subways" by Eve Mirriam (3)

"About Feet" by Margaret Hillert (3)

"The Sidewalk Racer" by Lillian Morrison (3)

"Jump-Jump-Jump" by Kate Greenaway (4)

"The Merry-Go-Round" by Myra Cohn Livingston (4)

"The Things I Do" by Karla Kuskin (5)

"Travel Plans" by Bobbie Katz (6)

"Song of the Train" by David McCord (11)

BOOKS ABOUT LOCOMOTION:

Roller Skates by Stephanie Calmenson

Harriet and the Roller Coaster by Nancy Carlson

The Perfect Ride by Lady McCrady

Shake My Sillies Out by Raffi

The Garden Walked Away by Elva Robinson

Freight Train by Donald Crews

Truck by Donald Crews

Airport by Byron Barton

The Little Engine That Could by Watty Piper

Trains at Work by Richard Ammon

Train Leaves the Station by Eve Merriam

From *Daily Poetry* published by GoodYearBooks. Copyright © 1995 Carol Simpson

EXTENDING ACTIVITIES

It is fun to observe the living things around us and discover how they move. This lesson not only touches on animal movement, but it also gives students a chance to talk about how people move. Yes, we walk and dance and run; but we also ride on planes, trains, boats, and cars, as well as use more exciting modes of transportation, such as the roller coaster. "Locomotion" and "Transportation" are the main themes of this lesson.

LETTER/SOUND ASSOCIATIONS: If you are going on a letter hunt, you will find all but the letters "j," "x," and "z" within the text of this poem. Present the "qu" sound, found in the word "squirrel." Talk about the double consonants in the words "padded," "squirrel," "wall," "wiggles," and "all" as having a single sound. The word "limb" has a silent "b" sound for those who are ready for this concept. The "aw" sound is featured in the words "paws" and "crawl."

RHYMING WORDS: Take a look at the pattern of lines that rhyme. In the first four lines we have an ABCB pattern. The next four lines are DEDE. The last four lines of print could be considered just two lines of the poem because they don't rhyme with the first four lines, when you take into account the rhythm that has been established. Look at spelling patterns that are the same as you underline the rhyming words with like marker colors. Most of the rhyming words are spelled similarly, except "swim" and "limb."

WORD FAMILIES: There are many word families that can be studied in the words of this poem. Here are two you might select to put on charts:

"ut" (but, cut, hut, shut, rut, nut, etc.)

"aw" (paw, draw, claw, straw, slaw, etc.)

VOCABULARY: Find the names of animals and circle or underline them. You can also identify the verb that is presented with each animal name. Ask your students to demonstrate the animal actions. Where do the animals go? How do they move around? The answers are, in some instances, prepositional phrases: "on padded paws," "from limb to limb," "up a wall," "by its tail," "upon the ground." What is another word that can replace "sail" to give it a clearer meaning? Take a look at the word "flies." How is the singular word spelled? Discuss the rule of dropping the "y" before adding the ending. Apply the rule to other words as examples. Does it apply to the word "monkey"? Why not?

SOCIAL STUDIES/SCIENCE: Brainstorm a list of human kinds of locomotion. Compare human locomotion to animal movement. Some animals can move in many ways, just as humans do. Animal movement depends upon the habitat in which the animal lives. Using a Venn Diagram, compare and contrast the ways animals move.

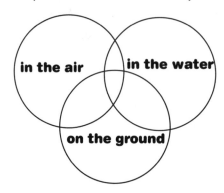

in the air · in the water · on the ground

Be sure to provide your students with plenty of nonfiction books on the subject of animals and locomotion. Small groups can get together and write reports about animals that fly, animals that swim, animals that hop, etc. Some may want to do a report on animals that move in more than one way. Let groups share their findings, make posters, and display their reports for others to see.

EXTEND WITH A BOOK: Most children enjoy going to the amusement park and riding on the roller coaster and the Ferris Wheel. Share *The Perfect Ride* by Lady McCrady. This book will get your students excited about discussing their favorite rides in the amusement park. Most have been to such a place and will be able to talk about the thrills they experienced there. You may want to list three or four rides and ask students to graph their favorite one. Here is an example.

ROLLER COASTER							
FERRIS WHEEL							
LOG RIDE							
SPOOK HOUSE							

CREATIVE WRITING: Extend the discussion of locomotion to include the students' favorite modes of child-oriented transportation. Items such as skateboards, bicycles, rollerblades, and battery powered all-terrain vehicles are popular with kids. When they get home from school and want to ride like the wind, what do they do? Where do they go? How does it feel when the wind tickles their face and messes up their hair? Do they like the feeling of going fast? Have them write about their favorite mode of transportation.

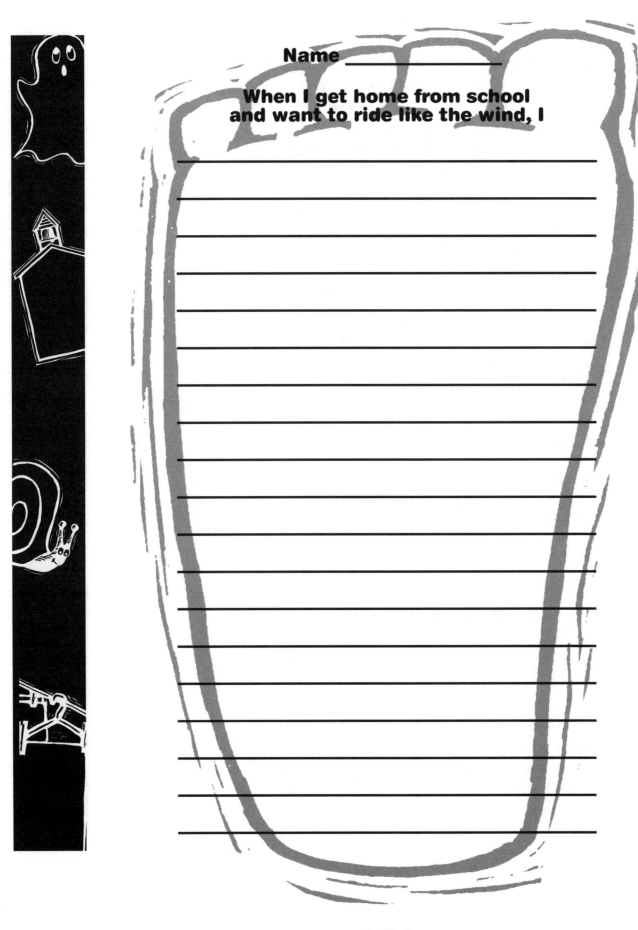

Name _____

**When I get home from school
and want to ride like the wind, I**

The Seed
by
Carol Simpson

I'm planting a seed.

I hope it will grow.

I'll water it carefully

And one day I know

That something will happen.

Just wait and see.

That tiny little seed

Will grow into a tree.

OTHER POEMS ABOUT SEEDS:

"A Pumpkin Seed" by Alice Crowell Hoffman (1)
"Tommy" by Gwendolyn Brooks (1, 4)
"The Sun" by Mary Lou Healy (1)
"Tiny Seeds" by Vera L. Stafford (1)
"Maytime Magic" by Mabel Watts (3)
"Birdseed" by Brod Bagert (20)

BOOKS ABOUT SEEDS:

The Carrot Seed by Ruth Krauss
Seeds and More Seeds by Millicent E. Selsam
Growing Vegetable Soup by Lois Ehlert
Planting a Rainbow by Lois Ehlert
The Reason for a Flower by Ruth Heller
Now I Know All About Seeds by Susan Kuchalla
The Seasons of Arnold's Apple Tree by Gail Gibbons
The Tiny Seed by Eric Carle
Corn Is Maize by Aliki
Pumpkin Pumpkin by Jeanne Titherington

From *Daily Poetry* published by GoodYearBooks. Copyright © 1995 Carol Simpson.

EXTENDING ACTIVITIES

"Seeds" is always a good theme to present in the spring when new life awakens all around us. But it is also a good topic for fall when squirrels can be seen carrying nuts (seeds) to bury for later. Some flowers drop their seeds to the ground when the weather turns cold. What happens to those seeds? During the winter, where do the seeds go? Are they dead? What brings them to life again? As you can see, a lesson about seeds might be appropriate at any time of the year.

LETTER/SOUND ASSOCIATIONS: This poem offers the opportunity to teach long and short vowel sounds, as most are represented. Talk about the long vowel rules as you present the words "hope," "seed," and others. The silent "k" in the word "know" can be discussed and other examples of that rule can be listed. The "ow" sound appears in "grow" and "know." Compare it to the same spelling but different sound in words such as "how," "now," and "brown." There are words that have an ending "y." What sound does that letter make in the words "carefully," "day," and "tiny"?

RHYMING WORDS: The two rhyming pairs ("grow"/"know" and "see"/"tree") have the same spelling patterns. Locate the rhyming words and underline or circle them with like marker colors. Note that rhyming words usually appear at the ends of the lines of the poem. The rhyming pattern in this piece is ABCBDEFE.

WORD FAMILIES: Two word families that are suggested for study here are:

"ing" (something, ring, wing, swing, bring, sing, thing, etc.)
"it" (it, sit, fit, hit, pit, bit, kit, etc.)

VOCABULARY: This poem contains contractions that you can break into the two words that were put together. Be sure to reread the poem with two words and see what happens to the rhythm. There are also compound words to locate and turn into two words. The speaker in this poem hopes the seed will grow into a tree. Replace the word "tree" at the end of the poem with other things that grow from seeds. Possibilities might include a tomato, rosebush, carrot, watermelon, and others. Write the suggestions on sticky notes and then you can easily change the ending of the poem by covering up the original word. Note that replacing the word will eliminate the rhyme, unless students can think of a word that not only fits the meaning but the rhyme as well. Take time to introduce the –fully suffix. What other words contain this suffix? Make a list. What other suffixes can your students name?

SCIENCE: Gather a selection of nonfiction books and materials so that students can do research on seeds. Bring in a variety of mystery seeds and try planting them. What grows? Discuss what the seeds need in order to grow. What will happen if they are deprived of sunlight, air, and water? How are seeds carried from place to place? Some seeds grow quickly, others take a long time. Make a list of plants that grow fast and slow. Sprinkle birdseed on a wet sponge and see what happens.

ART FROM A TRADE BOOK: Lois Ehlert's *Planting a Rainbow* or *Growing Vegetable Soup* can be the basis of a colorful garden picture. Have your students cut out plants and garden tools from large pieces of construction paper and make a class garden mural. Label the picture in the same way that Lois Ehlert labels everything on the pages of her books. Discuss the names of the tools you use in the garden and the function of each one.

CREATIVE WRITING: Assign the following for creative writing: On your way home from school you find a mysterious seed on the sidewalk. You take it home and plant it. What do you hope will grow? Write a story about your mystery seed. Where did you find it? Why did it catch your eye? Was it tiny or big? How do you take care of your seed?

Name_____

I found a seed on my way home from school._____

_____

_____

_____

_____

_____

_____

_____

_____

_____

_____

_____

_____

_____

_____

_____

_____

Who Has Seen the Wind?
by
Christina Rossetti

Who has seen the wind?

Neither I nor you.

But when the leaves hang trembling,

The wind is passing through.

Who has seen the wind?

Neither you nor I.

But when the trees bow down their heads,

The wind is passing by.

OTHER POEMS ABOUT WEATHER:

"The Friendly Shower" by Alice Thorn Frost (1)
"April Rain Song" by Langston Hughes (1, 2, 3, 4, 14)
"Wind Song" by Mimi Brodsky (1)
"Rainy Day" by Gina Bell-Zano (1)
"Start of a Storm" by Lou Ann Welte (1)
"So Long as There's Weather" by Tamara Kitt (2)
"Weather" by Eve Mirriam (2, 11, 14)
"Clouds" by Christina Rossetti (2, 14)
"Galoshes" by Rhoda Bacmeister (2)
"Rain" by Myra Cohn Livingston (2, 14)
"The Wind" by James Reeves (3)
"Fog" by Carl Sandburg (3)
"Weather" by Anonymous (3)
"Rain" by Robert Louis Stevenson (4, 5, 9, 14)
"Rain Sizes" by John Ciardi (5)
"Storm" by Roger McGough (8)
"Monsoon" by Alfreda de Silva (8)
"Hurricane" by James Berry (8)
"The Storm" by Julie Holder (8)

BOOKS ABOUT WEATHER:

Gilberto and the Wind by Marie Hall Ets
Storm by Seymour Simon
Rain by Barbara Hill
The Cloud Book by Tomie dePaola
The Storm Book by Charlotte Zolotow
A Rainbow of My Own by Don Freeman
The Wind Blew by Pat Hutchins
Weather Words by Gail Gibbons
Weather Forecasting by Gail Gibbons
Thunder Cake by Patricia Polacco
Peter Spier's Rain by Peter Spier
Peter and the North Wind retold by Freya Littledale
Listen to the Rain by Bill Martin, Jr. and John Archambault

EXTENDING ACTIVITIES

Everyone must face the weather everyday. Children are interested in, and have some understanding of, different kinds of weather. Whether it be sunny, rainy, cloudy, stormy, snowy, or windy, everyone deals with it in his or her own way. We dress for the weather. We prepare for a serious storm by boarding up the windows of our houses. We turn up the heat or turn on the air conditioning. Some places experience four distinct seasons, while others tend to be mostly warm or mostly cold. Use what children already know to help them learn more about weather and how people from other places deal with different kinds of storms. Weather is a topic that will vary from location to location because we all experience the wrath and blessings of Mother Nature in different ways. Be prepared with a selection of nonfiction books that explain weather phenomena of various kinds.

LETTER/SOUND ASSOCIATIONS: There are several spelling patterns that make a long "e" sound in this poem. Identify them and underline those words. Examples are the "ei" in "neither," the "ee" in "seen," and the "ea" in "leaves." You might wish to compare the word "leaves," which has the "ea" pattern with the word "head" which has the same "ea" pattern but a different sound. Make lists of other words with those two patterns and sounds. Here is an opportunity to look at words with the "ough" spelling such as "through." Other words with that spelling can be listed and sounds compared. ("though," "enough," "rough," "tough," "ought," "thought," etc.) Examine the "ow" sound in "bow" and "down." Compare it with the "ow" in "snow" or "grow."

RHYMING WORDS: The two intended rhyming pairs have different spelling patterns to discuss. You/through and I/by can be underlined with markers of two different colors. List other words that end in those spelling patterns. The ABCB pattern of rhyming is contained in both verses of the poem. Take note of the placement of rhyming words at the ends of lines of text.

WORD FAMILIES: Two word families suggested for further study are:

"ow" (bow, how, now, cow, plow, wow, etc.)
"y" (by, try, my, why, shy, fly, etc.)

VOCABULARY: Examine the either/or and neither/nor combinations. Notice the different meanings of the words. Ask students to explain the phrases, "the leaves hang trembling" and "the trees bow down their heads," in their own words. Replace the word "seen" with other appropriate ones, such as "heard," "felt," "touched," "smelled," and others. How do you know the wind is there?

SCIENCE/SOCIAL STUDIES: Look at maps of the United States and the World. Discuss the weather near the poles and near the Equator. What happens the farther you get from the Equator? Read nonfiction books to learn more about the weather in other regions. What is a tornado or a hurricane? Can you have them where you live? Why or why not? List the weather features you have in your own location. Watch the weather forecaster on television. Is there a pattern to the weather? Does it seem to come from a certain direction? Does your weather seem to follow the weather that someplace else had the day before? If possible, invite the weather forecaster to visit your school and tell about his or her job.

From *Daily Poetry* published by GoodYearBooks. Copyright © 1995 Carol Simpson.

EXTEND WITH A BOOK: Pat Hutchins has written a book called *The Wind Blew*. Share this book with your class. The story is about the things that the wind carried away. Ask your class to each participate in writing a page of a windy day story. Have them complete the following sentence and illustrate their idea.

The wind carried away my _____ .

A final page might contain everything the wind had taken away, after having perhaps landed in the branches of a tree. Combine the pages and bind them into a class book that can be checked out and taken home to share.

GRAPHING: Instead of selecting your favorite kind of weather, why not graph what your students consider to be the worst weather. The choices will depend upon the weather you experience where you live. You might have the students choose from rain, snow, ice, or extreme heat. If you have studied other serious weather phenomena from around the globe, you might wish to select from a hurricane, a monsoon, a tornado, a cyclone, or a blizzard. Why do students choose the answers they do? What is so bad about a _____?

CREATIVE WRITING: Discuss with your students the things that happen on a windy day. We know that kites fly best if there is a breeze. What else happens on windy days? What do they like to do on a windy day? Ask them to write a story about a windy day.

WRITE A POEM: This poem offers a distinct pattern that could be modified slightly and used to write a parody verse. Have the students use it to write about weather.

Who has seen the _____ ?
Perhaps you and I.

And when the _____,
The _____ is passing by.

EXAMPLE:

Who has seen the rain?
Perhaps you and I.
And when the rose is dripping wet,
The rain is passing by.

Name_____

On a windy day,_____

_____

_____

_____

_____

_____

_____

_____

_____

_____

_____

_____

_____

SEASONS AND HOLIDAYS

As the name implies, these poems are to be used when a season or the holiday arrives. There are poems for the four seasons plus seven holidays throughout the year. Should you feel the need to eliminate any religious holiday observances, you may elect to extend the subject of winter in order to keep from using the Christmas and Hanukkah poems. Extend the spring theme an extra week, and you can eliminate the Easter theme. It will be your decision what to do for the "Poem of the Week" at those times. You might try your hand at writing a simple poem about snow or a snowman, or about the arrival of spring flowers, bugs, and animals that have been absent from the neighborhood.

From *Daily Poetry* published by GoodYearBooks. Copyright © 1995 Carol Simpson.

In Autumn
by
Winifred C. Marshall

They're coming down in showers,

The leaves all gold and red;

They're covering the little flowers,

And tucking them in bed.

They've spread a fairy carpet

All up and down the street;

And when we skip along to school,

They rustle 'neath our feet.

OTHER POEMS ABOUT AUTUMN:

"Autumn" by Charlotte L. Riser (1)
"September" by Brierly Ashour (1)
"Leaf Blankets" by Irene B. Crofoot (1)
"October" by Winifred C. Marshall (1)
"Time to Play" by Ada Clark (1)
"Let the Fall Leaves Fall" by Clyde Watson (5)
"Autumn Fires" by Robert Louis Stevenson (9)

BOOKS ABOUT AUTUMN:

Wonders of the Season by Keith Brandt
The Apple Tree by Lynley Dodd
Goodbye Geese by Nancy White Carlstrom
I Can Read About Seasons by Robyn Supraner
The Seasons of Arnold's Apple Tree by Gail Gibbons
Johnny Appleseed by Steven Kellogg
Autumn Across America by Seymour Simon
Birches by Robert Frost
The Fall of Freddie the Leaf by Leo Buscaglia

From *Daily Poetry* published by GoodYearBooks. Copyright © 1995 Carol Simpson.

EXTENDING ACTIVITIES

Autumn, or fall, has a different look in various parts of the country. If you are living in a place where the trees turn brilliant colors in autumn, you and your children will be able to understand what the poet means when she writes about the leaves. If you do not live in a place with autumn leaves, you will want to find some magazine pictures or posters that show the beautiful colors. You may want to color scraps of paper in autumn colors, wrinkle them up, and throw them on the floor so that your students can pretend to experience the fun of walking and swishing through a pile of crisp dry leaves.

LETTER/SOUND ASSOCIATIONS: Look for words that have the two spelling patterns that make the "ow" sound ("down," "showers," "flowers," "our"). Make a list of other words with the same spelling and sound patterns. Compare "down" with the word own. Note the difference in the sound. The "th," "wh," and "sh" sounds can be located in words in this poem.

RHYMING WORDS: The rhyming pairs ("showers"/"flowers," "red"/"bed," and "street"/"feet") are made with matching spelling patterns. Take note of the placement of the words at the ends of the lines of print. The first four lines would seem to indicate an ABAB pattern to the poem. But, the second set of four lines switches to a CDED pattern instead.

WORD FAMILIES: Two word families that are suggested for further study at this time are:

"ip" (skip, tip, lip, flip, drip, rip, slip, etc.)

"old" (gold, told, fold, bold, scold, sold, etc.)

177

VOCABULARY: There are some interesting phrases in this poem that you may want to discuss. Ask your students what they think is meant by:

"coming down in showers"
"tucking them in bed"
"spread a fairy carpet"
"rustle 'neath our feet"

As suggested earlier, if your students do not have the opportunity to walk in the autumn leaves, you might want to make some out of scraps of typing paper. Then they will understand the "rustle 'neath our feet" phrase. Identify the two words that make up the contraction words "they're" and "they've." What is meant by the shortened word "'neath?" Find the color words in the poem. Mark them in the colors they name. What other colors do you think of in the autumn?

AUTUMN ART PROJECT: If you live in a location where you see the autumn leaves, gather some of them to press with crayon shavings. You will need waxed paper and an iron as well as leaves and crayon shavings to do this simple project. Spread the leaves on a piece of waxed paper. Sprinkle a rather generous handful of crayon shavings of many colors on top of and around the edges of the leaves. Place a second sheet of waxed paper on top and press with an iron set on a low setting. When the crayon shavings melt, they mix with the leaves and make a nice autumn print. Trim the waxed paper in unusual shapes that fit the outline of the leaves, and frame it with construction paper cut in the same unusual shape (one "frame" for the front of the waxed paper, and one "frame" for the reverse side). Hang your prints so that both sides can be seen.

From *Daily Poetry* published by GoodYearBooks. Copyright © 1995 Carol Simpson.

SCIENCE/HEALTH: Discuss the changes that come with autumn in your part of the world. List some of the signs of autumn that apply to you. Do you have to change your wardrobe to include long sleeves and long pants? Do you need to wear a jacket to stay healthy when you go outside? Do you see flocks of birds flying south for the winter? Take note of, and record, the temperature at a specific time every day to see how slowly or quickly the temperature goes down as winter approaches.

SCIENCE/MATH: There are many activities you can do with pumpkins at this time of the year. Buy several pumpkins of various sizes, from small to big. Let students guess the circumference of the biggest pumpkin by cutting a piece of string or yarn that they think will fit tightly around it. Hang up the pieces of string or yarn. Cut a piece that is the correct size and compare it to the guesses the students made. Another guessing activity involves the weight of the biggest pumpkin. Record all guesses on pieces of paper and arrange them in numerical sequence on a long sheet of oaktag or adding machine tape. Weigh the pumpkin and place the correct number along the sequential line of guesses. Compare those that were too light, too heavy, and almost right. Try a sinking/floating activity using the smallest pumpkin as well as items such as a coin, a cork, a pencil, an eraser, a sponge, and a variety of things that will sink or float. Leave the small pumpkin for last. Ask if it will sink to the bottom or stay afloat. Watch the look of surprise when it does not sink! Discover which way it floats—with stem up, sideways, or stem down. Try the same thing with the middle sized pumpkin. If you have a large enough tub, you can also float your biggest pumpkin. When you are ready to carve your pumpkins, count the seeds and put them in groups of ten. How many seeds did your biggest pumpkin have? Did it have the same number as the smallest? And, of course, you can bake the seeds and eat them as a final activity.

EXTEND WITH A BOOK: *The Fall of Freddie the Leaf* by Leo Buscaglia is an excellent book to demonstrate the association of death with autumn and rebirth with spring. Discuss the life cycle of the leaf and other living things.

GRAPHING: Have children graph their favorite season. Instead of coloring in a space or writing their name on the spaces, ask the students to draw a 3" x 3" picture of themselves doing something they like to do during their favorite season (suitable examples would include swimming, jumping in leaves, building a snowman, or picking a flower).

CREATIVE WRITING: Talk about the autumn season and what it means to you in your location. Brainstorm a list of things the students like to do in the fall. Ask students to pick one or two activities from the brainstorming list and write a story about an autumn day.

From *Daily Poetry* published by GoodYearBooks. Copyright © 1995 Carol Simpson.

Name _____

Autumn is a fun time to _____

_____

_____

_____

_____

_____

_____

_____

_____

_____

_____

_____

_____

_____

_____

_____

_____

First Snow
by
Marie Louise Allen

Snow makes whiteness where it falls,

The bushes look like popcorn balls.

The places where I always play

Look like somewhere else today.

From *Daily Poetry* published by GoodYearBooks. Copyright © 1995 Carol Simpson.

OTHER POEMS ABOUT WINTER:

"Winter Pleasures" by Nona Keen Duffy (1)
"A Winter Inn" by Authur Wallace Peach (1)
"Firewood" by Julia W. Wolfe (1)
"Winter Night" by Claude Weimer (1)
"Snowfall" by Margaret Hillert (1)
"Crumbs On the Snow" by Lucretia Penny (1)
"Let's Go Coasting" by Nona Keen Duffy (1)
"I Heard a Bird Sing" by Oliver Herford (2, 3, 14)
"Dragon Smoke" by Lilian Moore (2, 14)
"Stopping By Woods on a Snowy Evening"
by Robert Frost (2, 3, 14)
"January" by John Updike (3)
"Smells" by Kathryn Worth (3)
"When" by Dorothy Aldis (3)
"First Snow" by Aileen Fisher (5)
"Calling" by Wes Magee (7)
"Snow" by Richard Edwards (8)
"Snowman" by Shel Silverstein (21)

BOOKS ABOUT WINTER:

The Mystery of the Missing Red Mitten by Steven Kellogg
January Brings the Snow by Sara Coleridge
The Snowball War by Bernice Chardiet and
Grace Maccarone
The Snow Kept on Falling by Kathie McQueary
White Snow, Bright Snow by Alvin Tresselt
A Wintery Day by Douglas Florian
Katy and the Big Snow by Virginia Lee Burton
Thomas' Snowsuit by Robert Munsch
The Mitten by Alvin Tresselt
The Mitten by Jan Brett
The Snowy Day by Ezra Jack Keats
The Big Snow by Berta and Elmer Hader
When Winter Comes by Robert Maass
Dear Rebecca, Winter Is Here by Jean Craighead George

EXTENDING ACTIVITIES

As with the autumn poem and activities, it is easier to understand what the winter season holds if you live somewhere that experiences snow. If not, you will need to get posters and/or magazine pictures that show snow coating the ground, clinging to the limbs of trees, and sitting on top of fenceposts. You may want to do a winter lesson in January when the holidays have ended and you have a week to look at seasonal changes.

LETTER/SOUND ASSOCIATIONS: Take a look at the "s" and "es" plural suffixes that are represented in this poem. Find every letter "s" in the poem. Use two marker colors to distinguish those that are used to represent the plural form of a noun and those that are the "s" ending of a present tense verb. Introduce "ness" as a suffix in the word "whiteness." List other words that end with this suffix.

RHYMING WORDS: All four lines contain rhyming words at the end. The two pairs of rhyming words have matching spelling patterns. List other words that are also spelled in that way. Note the AABB rhyming pattern.

WORD FAMILIES: Two word families that you might wish to study further are:

"ook" (look, book, cook, hook, shook, brook, etc.)
"all" (fall, ball, call, wall, hall, tall, small, etc.)

From *Daily Poetry* published by GoodYearBooks. Copyright © 1995 Carol Simpson.

VOCABULARY: What does the poet mean when she uses the word "whiteness"? How can bushes look like popcorn balls? Look for compound words and highlight them. On sticky notes, write the two words that were combined to make one word.

SNOWFLAKE ART: Make a snowflake mobile. Cut snowflakes out of white typing paper. Tissue paper folds and cuts easily, but it does not hold its shape the way typing paper does when hung in a mobile. If you do use tissue paper, try mounting your cut snowflakes on blue construction paper. If it is a snowy day, go outside and have the students collect snowflakes on their mittens or gloves and look closely at the different patterns. Students should make a variety of snowflake patterns in their artwork.

TORN PAPER ART: Tear sheets of white typing paper into tiny pieces. Have students glue the tiny pieces on a dark blue or black background to make a snow picture. You might suggest making a torn paper snowman or snowfort, or depicting children throwing snowballs or making snow angels.

SCIENCE: Discuss the plight of the winter birds that inhabit your neighborhood. Suggest making a bird feeder out of a milk carton. Cut a hole in the side and put birdseed inside. Hang your bird feeder in a nearby tree and watch for the birds to come and eat.

SOCIAL STUDIES: Look at a world globe. Locate the poles and Equator. What happens to the weather the closer you get to the poles? Listen to the weather forecaster. Record the daily temperature at a specific time to note how it is dropping or rising as the days go by.

EXTEND WITH A BOOK: Read the two listed versions of *The Mitten* by Jan Brett and Alvin Tresselt. Compare and contrast the two stories. How are they alike? How are they different? Graph the students' favorite version.

GRAPHING: Have the students graph the answer to this question: Do you wear a pair of mittens or do you wear a pair of gloves? Give students small pieces of paper (about 5" x 5") and let them cut out a mitten or glove to place on a graph. Be sure to examine and measure the results of your graph.

CREATIVE WRITING: Use the following scenario for creative writing: Imagine spending an afternoon building a big snowman. You take your time making the snowballs just right. You find just the right sticks for its arms. You borrow your mother's best scarf to put around its neck. You sneak into the kitchen and get a bright orange carrot for a nose and a handful of little cookies to make eyes, a mouth, and buttons. Your snowman is perfect! At bedtime, you hear a noise coming from your front yard. Your snowman is waking up for the night! Your snowman is off on an adventure. Write about the adventure.

Name_____

At night, my snowman went on a big adventure!

_____
_____
_____
_____
_____
_____
_____
_____
_____
_____
_____
_____
_____
_____
_____

Conn

The Worm
by
Ralph Bergengren

When the earth is turned in spring
The worms are fat as anything.

And birds come flying all around
To eat the worms right off the ground.

They like worms just as much as I
Like bread and milk and apple pie.

And once, when I was very young,
I put a worm right on my tongue.

I didn't like the taste a bit,
And so I didn't swallow it.
But oh, it makes my Mother squirm
Because she thinks I ate that worm!

"The Worm" from *Jane, Joseph, and John* by Ralph Bergengren.
Reprinted by permission of Little, Brown and Company.

From *Daily Poetry* published by GoodYearBooks. Copyright © 1995 Carol Simpson.

OTHER POEMS ABOUT SPRING:

"Good-By and Hello!" by Barbara Anthony (1)
"March" by Mildred Pittinger (1)
"Spring's Magic" by Faye Tanner Cool (1)
"March Wind" by Eleanor Dennis (1)
"It's Spring" by Winnifred J. Mott (1)
"To a Red Kite" by Lillian Moore (2, 14)
"Spring" by Karla Kuskin (3)
"Spring Rain" by Marchette Chute (3)
"Spring Again" by Karla Kuskin (4)
"When Spring Appears" by Jean Kenward (7)

BOOKS ABOUT SPRING:

Waiting for Spring Stories by Bethany Roberts
Now I Know Changing Seasons by Rose Greydanus
The Garden Walked Away by Elva Robinson
Now I Know—Look—A Butterfly by David Cutts
Wake Up Bear by Lynley Dodd
Trees by Harry Behn
A Tree Is Nice by Janice May Udry

EXTENDING ACTIVITIES

Spring is a time of new life. It is a time to greet the birds and the green grass and worms once again. This poem presents a humorous look at some of the signs of spring. Children will wiggle and squirm as they try to imagine eating a worm!

LETTER/SOUND ASSOCIATIONS: If you are still identifying letters of the alphabet, you will find all but "x" and "z" in this poem. Because the letter "q" is included, you can introduce the idea that 'u" almost always follows "q" in words. You can locate the letter "c" when it appears and identify it as a soft "s" or hard "k" sound. You may want to present the "sh," "ch," "th," and "wh" sounds in this poem. The words "apple," "all," and "swallow" contain double consonants that make single sounds. Say the poem slowly. See how many different spellings of the "er" (as in "her") sound you can identify ("worms," "earth," "squirm," "birds").

RHYMING WORDS: Each pair of lines contains a rhyme and half have identical spelling patterns. Locate and underline all rhyming pairs, noting their placement at the ends of the lines of print. Take a look at the pairs with unmatched spelling patterns and try to list other words with those same patterns. Remember to underline each of the rhyming pairs with a different marker color so that you can show the AABBCCDDEEFF pattern in the poem with the use of Unifix® Cubes.

From *Daily Poetry* published by GoodYearBooks. Copyright © 1995 Carol Simpson.

WORD FAMILIES: Two suggested word families to explore further at this time are:

"ate" (ate, date, late, plate, state, fate, rate, etc.)

"ound" (ground, around, found, sound, pound, etc.)

VOCABULARY: Locate the contraction word in the poem. You can find it twice. Write the two words on sticky notes to show how they are put together to make the contraction. Change the word "ate" in the last line of the poem to other appropriate words. You might try the words "bit," "chewed," "swallowed," or "liked." Note that the word you use to replace "ate" needs to be in the past tense. Here is an opportunity to discuss the present tense of the other verbs in the poem. Students can think of other foods to replace the words "bread and milk." By leaving "apple pie" in place, you do not affect the rhyme.

ART PROJECT: This poem is fun to illustrate. Give students a uniform size piece of plain paper (6″ x 6″ is good) to draw their own faces and tongues with a worm. Mount the illustrations around your poetry chart on a bulletin board for others to see.

ART/SCIENCE: Brainstorm a list of signs of spring. Draw small 3″ x 3″ pictures of your signs of spring and hang them on hangers to make a seasonal mobile, in the same manner as the one described in the School lesson.

EXTEND WITH A BOOK: Share the book *Wake Up Bear* by Lynley Dodd. What was the bear doing? What did the other animals do to try to wake him up? What finally did wake him up? Ask students what it takes to awaken them from a deep sleep. Write a class story in which each student contributes a page that completes the following sentence and also contains an appropriate illustration. Bind pages together in a book.

To wake me up you must_____.

MORE SPRING SCIENCE: Discuss the spring equinox and what it means. Use a flashlight and globe to demonstrate the concept. Watch for the arrival of spring birds and bugs. Keep track on a calendar or time line. Record daily temperatures at a specific time and watch for fluctuations and steadily rising readings.

CREATIVE WRITING: If your climate is such that you experience a cold winter season, the arrival of spring usually means that your children cannot wait to get outside once again and play. Ask them to write a story about what they can do on a nice spring day.

Name _____

Oh, boy! Warm weather is coming! Now I can

_____
_____
_____
_____
_____
_____
_____
_____
_____
_____
_____
_____
_____
_____
_____
_____

Summer's End
by
Judith Viorst

One by one the petals drop.

There's nothing that can make them stop.

You cannot beg a rose to stay.

Why does it have to be that way?

The butterflies I used to chase

Have gone off to some other place.

I don't know where. I only know

I wish they didn't have to go.

And all the shiny afternoons

So full of birds and big balloons

And ice cream melting in the sun

Are done. I do not want them done.

From *Daily Poetry* published by GoodYearBooks. Copyright © 1995 Carol Simpson.

OTHER POEMS ABOUT SUMMER:

"Sing a Song of Summer" by Kay Winters (1)
"Summer's Invitation" by Lelend B. Jacobs (1)
"School" by Iva Riebel Judy (1)
"Going Fishing" by Solveig Paulson Russell (1)
"August" by John Updike (3)
"I Woke Up in the Morning" by Sonja Dunn (17)

BOOKS ABOUT SUMMER:

The Cut-Ups at Camp Custer by James Marshall
Amelia Bedelia Goes Camping by Peggy Parish
Roller Skates by Stephanie Calmenson
Little Critter's The Trip by Mercer Mayer
Christina Katerina and the Box by Patricia Lee Gauch
The Perfect Ride by Lady McCrady
Runaway Ralph by Beverly Cleary
Three by the Sea by James Marshall
Four on the Shore by James Marshall
When Summer Ends by Susi Gregg Fowler
A Time of Wonder by Robert McCloskey
Arthur Goes to Camp by Marc Brown
When Summer Comes by Robert Maass

EXTENDING ACTIVITIES

This poem is written as a reflection on the end of summer rather than as a celebration of the beginning of summer vacation. For this reason, it is suggested that you include this lesson near the beginning, if not the first week, of the new school year. Students can reflect on their past summer vacation and on what they did. If you will look at the list of "Other Poems," you may find one more suited to the idea of summer's coming, if that is your preference.

LETTER/SOUND ASSOCIATIONS: If this poem is used early in the school year, you will want to go on a letter hunt with your emergent readers. You can find all letters except "j," "q," "x," and "z." Ask students to find a letter that makes the "p-p-p" sound (or another appropriate sound) if you are ready to isolate sounds as well as letters. With your older readers, you can compare the word "butterflies" with the singular noun "butterfly. "Notice the change in the letter "y" before making the word plural. There are opportunities to discuss all five short vowel sounds and all five long vowel sounds as well. Double letters that make single sounds can be pointed out in the words "cannot," "butterflies," "off," "all," "afternoons," and "balloons." Hard "k" and soft "s" sounds of the letter "c" can be presented. The letter/sound activities you do will depend upon the level of your students.

RHYMING WORDS: There are six pairs of rhyming words to locate and circle or underline in various marker colors. Using Unifix® Cubes of the same colors, you can arrange and visualize the AABB pattern of each of the three verses. Be sure to look at the differences in spelling patterns in some of the rhyming pairs and try to list other words with those same spelling variations.

From *Daily Poetry* published by GoodYearBooks. Copyright © 1995 Carol Simpson.

WORD FAMILIES: If you are beginning the year with this poem and you are working with pre-emergent readers, you may elect to wait until later to begin introducing the concept of word families. If your students understand the concept, you might want to introduce and chart the following:

"ish" (wish, dish, fish, swish, etc.)
"eg" (beg, leg, peg, keg, etc.)

VOCABULARY: There are three contraction words to identify and turn into two whole words. Look for the nouns that name summertime things. Talk about the tone of sadness in this poem. Is the end of summer a sad time or a happy time for your students? Younger children may not understand the word "petals" and may need an explanation. There are several compound words that can be identified and turned into two words.

EXTEND WITH A BOOK: Patricia Lee Gauch's book *Christina Katerina and the Box* is a story that presents a fanciful look at the many uses of big boxes. Share the story with your students. Sequence the events in order. Nearly everyone at some time will have had the thrill of turning a big box into a castle or a racecar. Talk about boxes and what you can do with them. Let everyone draw a picture and write or dictate a sentence that begins:

I turned my big box into a _____.

Put all the pictures and sentences together into a book that can be checked out and shared at home. Emergent readers will enjoy and feel successful sharing this repetitive sentence.

CREATIVE WRITING: Use the following for a creative writing activity: Think back on one of the hottest days of the summer. What did you do to stay cool when the temperature outside was at its hottest? Write a story about keeping cool.

SCIENCE: When summer comes to an end, there are temperature changes. Keep track of the temperature each day at a specific time and record on a calendar or time line. Note the steady drop from the beginning of school until the middle to end of October. When did it stop feeling like summer and begin feeling like autumn?

Name_____

The best way to keep cool on a hot summer day is to _____

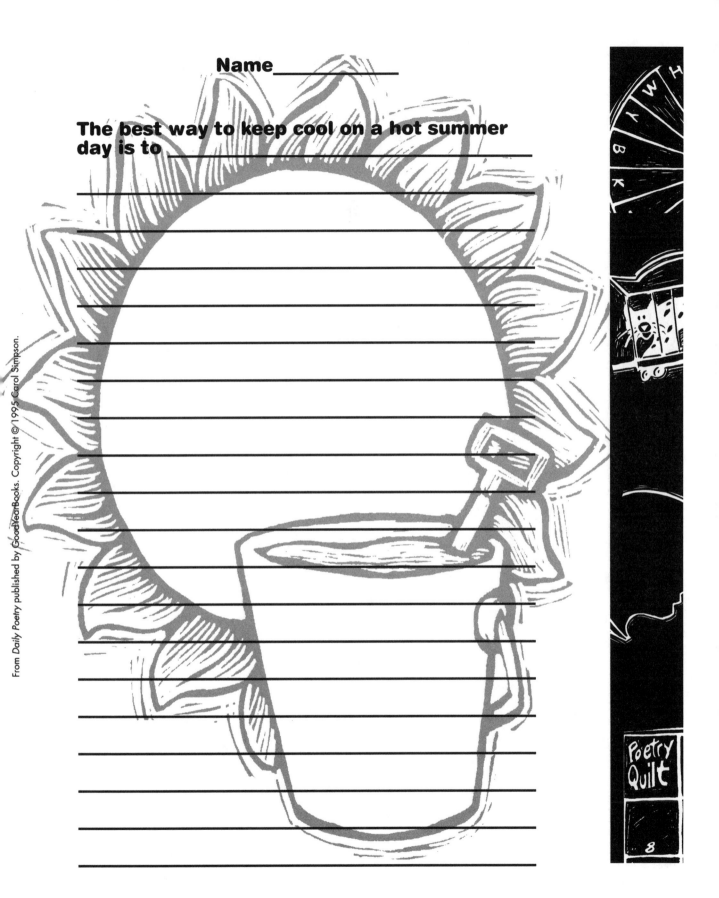

Poetry Quilt

8

Hallowe'en Parade
by
Sonja Dunn

Witches, goblins, skeletons, ghosts,

Tell us the costume you love most.

Black cat

Fat cat

Hissing at the moon

Black cat

Scary cat

Riding on a broom

Black cat

Fat bat

Spider toad

Hallowe'en parade

Comin' down the road

From *Daily Poetry* published by GoodYearBooks. Copyright © 1995 Carol Simpson.

OTHER POEMS ABOUT HALLOWEEN:

"Halloween Fun" by Fern Curtis (1)
"Look at That" by Lilian Moore (1)
"On Halloween Night" by Ruth Linsley Forman (1)
"The Jack-o'-Lantern" by Florence Lind (1)
"The Old Wife and the Ghost" by James Reeves (2, 14)
"The Pumpkin" by Robert Graves (2, 3, 14)
"This is Halloween" by Dorothy Brown Thompson (3)
"Witches' Menu" by Sonja Nikolay (3)
"Halloween" by Ivy O. Eastwickk (4)
"Jack-o'-Lantern" by Aileen Fisher (5)
"In a Dark, Dark Wood" by Anonymous (5)
"The Witch's Brew" by Wes Magee (7)
"Hallowe'en" by Jean Kenward (7)
"Haunted House" by Jack Prelutsky (7)
"The Goblin" by Jack Prelutsky (7)
"Ghost" by Jack Prelutsky (7)
"Crazy Daddy" by Brod Bagert (19)

BOOKS ABOUT HALLOWEEN:

How Spider Saved Halloween by Robert Kraus
The Thirteen Days of Halloween by Carol Greene
Witches Four by Marc Brown
Scary, Scary Halloween by Eve Bunting
Who Goes Out on Halloween? by Sue Alexander
Old Old Witch by Bill Martin, Jr.
Little Witch's Big Night by Deborah Hautzig
Arthur's Halloween by Marc Brown
The Spooky Halloween Party by Annabelle Prager
Halloween with Morris and Boris by Bernard Wiseman
The Magic Pumpkin by Lucille E. Sette
Hallowhat? by Alan Benjamin
Dracula by Keith Faulkner

EXTENDING ACTIVITIES

There are so many stories and poems about this holiday. It seems to be a favorite time of the year for youngsters. Children will enjoy using their imaginations for the activities in this lesson.

LETTER/SOUND ASSOCIATIONS: This is a good poem for presenting or extending the short a sound. Look also at the "oo" sound in broom and moon. Look at the -ing suffix in "riding" and "hissing" as compared to the word "comin'." What word does the poet intend us to understand in the word "comin'"? Look for words that contain the long "i" sound. There are several blends to discover and discuss ("sp," "sk," "st").

RHYMING WORDS: This poem has a different rhyming pattern which can be identified more easily if you will use the Unifix® Cubes "trick" described earlier. It is important to present the idea that not all verses need to contain the same number of lines, nor the same kind of rhyming pattern. Underline the words that rhyme and look at spelling patterns that are alike and different. The words "ghosts/most" have a more subtle rhyme. The word "cat" appears many times in the poem, always at the end of a line of print, so that it presents rhyming pairs.

WORD FAMILIES: Two word families that might be presented at this time are:

"ell" (tell, bell, well, spell, shell, fell, smell, etc.)

"at" (cat, bat, rat, sat, fat, hat, that, chat, etc.)

VOCABULARY: Find all the nouns that name kinds of Halloween costumes. Replace the word "comin'" with other "ing" verbs such as "riding," "dancing," or "parading." Think of other words that describe a Halloween cat besides black, scary, and fat. You might change the descriptive words that are repeated in the last verse and replace them with "spooky" or "howling" or "tricky." See what other words you can come up with that describe cats on Halloween.

GRAPHING: Ask each student to draw a pumpkin face on a small piece of plain paper about 3" x 3" in size. Do not suggest kinds of faces that you find on jack-o'-lanterns. After drawings are completed, graph the results. Students must glue their jack-o'-lantern face into the appropriate space on the graph. Try the following format:

MY JACK-O'-LANTERN'S FACE IS:							
SCARY							
FUNNY							
HAPPY							
SAD							

From *Daily Poetry* published by GoodYearBooks. Copyright © 1995 Carol Simpson.

REWRITE A FAMILIAR STORY: Everyone knows "The Twelve Days of Christmas." Look for *The Thirteen Days of Halloween* by Carol Greene. This book provides a good model for creating your own classroom version for Halloween. Ask students to supply you with the ideas for gifts "my good friend gave to me," up to any number you select. Here are some examples:

1 - black cat in a bare tree
2 - spooky ghosts
3 - spider webs
4 - flying bats
5 - skeletons
6 - haunted houses
7 - trick-or-treaters
8 - bags of candy

ILLUSTRATE THE POEM: Have the students draw and cut out a large-sized picture of themselves in their Halloween costume. Display the drawings in a long line, as if in a parade.

CREATIVE WRITING: Talk about Halloween costumes. Some are scary, some are pretty, some are funny. Many students make their costumes from things they have around the house. Others buy their costumes from the store. Get your students to talk about some of the favorite costumes they have worn or seen in past Halloween parades. Ask them to write stories about their favorite costumes.

Name_____

I have a favorite costume. It is a

All In a Word
by
Aileen Fisher

T for time to be together
turkey, talk, and tangy weather.

H for harvest stored away,
home, and hearth, and holiday.

A for autumn's frosty art,
and abundance in the heart.

N for neighbors, and November,
nice things, new things to remember.

K for kitchen, kettles' croon,
kith and kin expected soon.

S for sizzles, sights, and sounds,

and something special that abounds.

That spells THANKS—for joy in living

and a jolly good Thanksgiving.

OTHER POEMS ABOUT THANKSGIVING:

"Glad Thanksgiving Day" by Effie Crawford (1)
"Were You Afraid?" by Beryl Frank (1)
"A Child's Song" by Alice F. Green (1)
"A Thanksgiving Dinner" by Maude M. Grant (1)
"Thanksgiving Day" by L. Maria Child (3, 4)
"Thanksgiving" by Ivy O. Eastwick (3)
"Turkey Time" by Sonja Dunn (18)
"I'm Thankful" by Jack Prelutsky (22)

BOOKS ABOUT THANKSGIVING:

It's Thanksgiving by Jack Prelutsky
I Can Read About the First Thanksgiving by J. I. Anderson
The First Thanksgiving by Linda Hayward
If You Sailed on the Mayflower by Ann McGovern
Children of the Earth and Sky by Stephen Krensky
The Legend of Indian Paintbrush by Tomie DePaola
Sarah Morton's Day by Kate Waters
Samuel Eaton's Day by Kate Waters
Dancing with the Indians by Angela Shelf Medearis
Clifford's Thanksgiving Visit by Norman Bridwell
How Many Days to America? by Eve Bunting
The Legend of Bluebonnet by Tomie DePaola
Three Young Pilgrims by Cheryl Harness
Hiawatha by Henry Wadsworth Longfellow
The Rough-Face Girl by Rafe Martin
A Turkey for Thanksgiving by Eve Bunting

EXTENDING ACTIVITIES

The Thanksgiving holiday is an appropriate time to learn about the Pilgrims and their journey on the Mayflower. There are many good books about the first Thanksgiving celebration and the people who attended. Here is an opportunity to talk about Native Americans and enjoy some of their legends and customs.

LETTER/SOUND ASSOCIATIONS: There are six obvious beginning letter sounds ("T"-"H"-"A"-"N"-"K"-"S") that could be expanded upon, as your students try to think of other things for which they might be thankful. Underline all the "t" words in the first two lines, all the "h" words in the second pair of lines, the "a" words in the third pair, and so on.

RHYMING WORDS: Each pair of lines contains rhyming words at the ends. As you underline the pairs of words in the same marker color, be sure to look at any differences in spelling patterns.

WORD FAMILIES: Two word families that are suggested for teaching in conjunction with this poem are:

"ood" (good, wood, hood, stood, etc.)
"oy" (joy, boy, toy, enjoy, employ, Roy, soy, etc.)

VOCABULARY: Depending upon the level of your students, you may find it necessary to look at meanings for some of the unusual words used in this poem. Explore also your students' understanding of the phrases "autumn's frosty art" or "tangy weather." This poem presents numerous opportunities to temporarily replace unknown words with ones that are more easily understood. For example, replace the word "croon" with the word sing; replace the word "kin" with the word relatives.

EXTEND WITH A BOOK: Read the two books by Kate Waters that tell about Pilgrim children, namely *Sarah Morton's Day* and *Samuel Eaton's Day.* Using a Venn Diagram or other comparison/contrast format, look at the lives of these two Pilgrim children. How do they compare with children's lives today? What are the differences and similarities? Would your students like to have lived during the early 1600s?

SOCIAL STUDIES/CREATIVE WRITING: There are many new trade books now available that tell Native American legends. Select several of them to share with your students. Encourage the children to think of an animal and to try to write their own legend about it. Perhaps students could work together in small groups to write and illustrate their legends.

ART PROJECTS ARE PLENTIFUL: From making feather headbands (don't forget to tell how you earned each feather) to constructing fringed vests out of grocery bags, from creating totem poles out of oatmeal boxes to cutting Pilgrim hats for boys and girls, the art projects for this holiday time are many and varied. If you do an extensive Thanksgiving unit, you may want to add making necklaces out of macaroni and noodles or clay beads to the above projects. Also consider candle-making. Or keep it simple and just have the students draw a picture of something for which they are thankful!

From *Daily Poetry* published by GoodYearBooks. Copyright © 1995 Carol Simpson.

MATH MEASUREMENT: There is much good literature about the Mayflower and its size. Using 12" long foot shapes cut out of construction paper (you will need about 140 of them), measure the approximate size of the little ship in a large room (a gymnasium is good). Line up your measuring "feet" to show the length and width. Then use string or yarn to outline the size of the deck. Invite 100 or more students to "Come aboard!" and they will discover just how crowded the Pilgrims would have been. As your students sit on the boat, be sure to enlighten them about the hazards of the long journey the Pilgrims made, and why they made such a dangerous trip. Share a book such as *If You Sailed On The Mayflower* by Ann McGovern.

MAKE A CLASS BOOK: Each child can contribute a page to a collection of "I am thankful for..." pages. The page should include an appropriate illustration. See if you can find a Thanksgiving bulletin board decoration that is an easy shape to cut, such as a cornucopia. When you give students their page to do, give them a cornucopia shaped page. Instead of a rectangular book, you can make a book of unusual shape. Use the decoration for your cover.

NAME ACROSTICS: The format of the poem for this week takes the six letters in the word "Thanks" and lists things that begin with these letters for which we might be thankful. Ask students to write down the letters of their first name and to turn these into thankful acrostics. Here is an example:

        F - food and friends
        R - rivers and roses
        A - animals and artists
        N - neighbors and night time
        K - kittens and kites

CREATIVE WRITING: Use the following for a creative writing activity: Imagine being a child on the Mayflower. After having studied books and nonfiction materials about the ship and its journey, write a story about making such a trip. What hardships did you encounter? Who were your friends? What did you do all day? Tell about your family. Why did you leave your home for a new land?

Name_____

I was a passenger on the Mayflower.
What an adventure that was! _____

From *Daily Poetry* published by GoodYearBooks. Copyright © 1995 Carol Simpson.

Poetry Quilt

8

Day Before Christmas
by
Marchette Chute

We have been helping with the cake

And licking out the pan,

And wrapping up our packages

As neatly as we can.

And we have hung our stockings up

Beside the open grate.

And now there's nothing more to do

Except

to

wait!

"Day Before Christmas" from *Rhymes About The Country* by Marchette Chute. Published 1941 by the Macmillan Company. Copyright © renewed 1969 by Marchette Chute. Reprinted by permission of Elizabeth Roach.

OTHER POEMS ABOUT CHRISTMAS:

"That Christmas Feeling" by Jane W. Krows (1)
"Bundles" by John Farrar (1)
"Busy" by Leland B. Jacobs (1)
"Christmas in the City" by Jean Brabham McKinney (1)
"Before Christmas" by Aileen Fisher (1)
"Christmas Tree" by Marion Edey (5)
"Ho, Ho, Ho" by Sonja Dunn (18)
"Jingle Bell Moose" by Sonja Dunn (18)
"Santa and the Reindeer" by Shel Silverstein (21)

BOOKS ABOUT CHRISTMAS:

It's Christmas by Jack Prelutsky
That's Not Santa by Leonard Kessler
How the Grinch Stole Christmas by Dr. Seuss
Harold at the North Pole by Crockett Johnson
The Story of Holly and Ivy by Rumer Godden
The Polar Express by Chris Van Allsburg
Hobo Dog's Christmas Tree by Thacher Hurd
The Christmas Witch by Stephen Kellogg
Claude the Dog, A Christmas Story by Dick Gackenbach
The Night Before Christmas by Clement C. Moore
Arthur's Christmas Cookies by Lillian Hoban
Arthur's Christmas by Marc Brown
Morris's Disappearing Bag by Rosemary Wells
Merry Christmas, Amelia Bedelia by Peggy Parish
Twelve Days of Christmas by Jack Kent
Merry Christmas, Mom and Dad by Mercer Mayer

EXTENDING ACTIVITIES

The week before Christmas (winter) vacation is a good time to talk about being patient. As the poem suggests, "and now there's nothing more to do except to wait!" It is difficult to keep composed at this time. Children are very excited about the coming holiday. Take this time to enjoy the wealth of poems and stories about Christmas.

LETTER/SOUND ASSOCIATIONS: Take a look at words containing the short vowel sounds; all five short vowel sounds are included. The long vowels "a," "e," "i," and "o" can be found. Look at the CVC, CVVC, CVCe configurations in some of the words. Compare the root words "help," "lick," and "wrap" with "helping," "licking," and "wrapping." Use this chance to teach the rule of doubling the consonant before adding a suffix to a short vowel word.

RHYMING WORDS: If you look at the first four lines of the poem you will notice the ABCB rhyming pattern. This pattern can be shown using Unifix® Cubes. As you read the poem for a second or third time, let students chime in on the second word of a rhyming pair. Stop and ask, "What two words sounded alike?" The second pair of rhyming words ("grate"/"wait") have different spelling patterns. You might want to list other ways to make the long a sound besides "a-e" and "ai."

WORD FAMILIES: Two word families that can be introduced in context and then expanded onto charts are:

"ap" (wrap, map, nap, snap, cap, tap, clap, etc.)
"ore" (more, store, shore, score, core, bore, chore, etc.)

VOCABULARY: Find and mark the phrases that describe what the poet does at Christmas time. Brainstorm a list of other things you must do to prepare for this holiday time. Sort or graph the phrases from the poem and your brainstorming list into two types: things you like to do and those you do not like to do.

EXTEND WITH A BOOK: Share the story of *The Polar Express* by Chris Van Allsburg, but do not show the pictures. Children can picture the story in their own minds. After they have heard the story, ask students to draw a picture of their favorite part. Note how closely they portray what the author/illustrator put in the book. Students can write or dictate a sentence that tells about their picture. If appropriate, organize the pictures in sequence and make your own class book of this favorite Christmas story. Share the original illustrations in Chris Van Allsburg's book before putting it away.

SOCIAL STUDIES: Gather the necessary nonfiction materials and present some Christmas traditions from places around the world. If, in your school, you have families that celebrate Christmas in different ways, ask a family member to come to your classroom and share some of their traditions.

BUILD THE POEM: Make flashcards of the lines or individual words of the poem. Let students go to a pocket chart and try to put the lines or words in proper sequence in order to build the poem. This can be done either as an individual or group activity. If you elect to do it with a group, you will probably want to use flashcards with words rather than with lines of the poem. Distribute the word cards as evenly as you can. As the poetry chart is read, students can arrange the word cards in the pocket chart in the same sequence. This activity encourages following along so that students' peers do not have to tell them that it's their turn to put in a word.

CREATIVE WRITING: Ask the students to write a story about the following: Make a Christmas wish list. Now imagine that of all the things on your list you will only get one. What one thing would you really want for Christmas?

Name _____

All I really want for Christmas is _____

Dreidel Song
by
Efraim Rosenzweig

Twirl about, dance about,

Spin, spin, spin!

Turn, Dreidel, turn—

Time to begin!

Soon it is Hanukkah—

Fast, Dreidel, fast!

For you will lie still

When Hanukkah's past.

From *Daily Poetry* published by GoodYearBooks. Copyright © 1995 Carol Simpson.

"Dreidel Song" from *Now We Begin* by Efraim Rosenzweig, 1937.
Reprinted by permission of the Union of Hebrew Congregations.

OTHER POEMS ABOUT HANUKKAH:

"Hanukkah Rainbow" by Eva Grant (1)
"At Hanukkah" by Vivian Gouled (1)
"Family Hanukkah" by Eva Grant (1)
"Joyous Hanukkah" by Eva Grant (1)
"Hanukkah Harmonica" by Mimi Brodsky (1)
"Light the Festive Candles" by Aileen Fisher (3)
"Hanukkah Candles" by Margaret Hillert (4)
"Eight Are the Lights" by Ilo Orleans (15)

BOOKS ABOUT HANUKKAH:

Hanukkah Lights, Hanukkah Nights by Leslie Kimmelman
Happy Hanukkah Rebus by David A. Adler
A Picture Book of Hanukkah by David A. Adler
Hershel and the Hanukkah Goblins by Trina Schart Hyman
Songs of Chanukah by Jeanne Modesitt
In the Month of Kislev: A Story for Hanukkah by Nina Jaffe
Hanukkah, Oh Hanukkah! compiled by Wendy Wax
The Gift by Aliana Brodman
Beni's First Chanukah by Jane Breskin Zalben
Hanukkah and Christmas at My House by Susan Enid Gertz

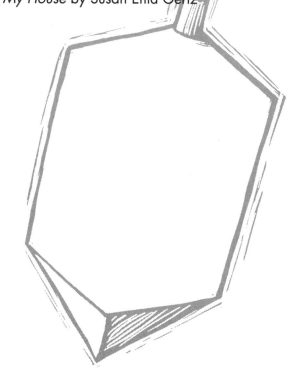

EXTENDING ACTIVITIES

This poem of the week is presented in addition to, or, if appropriate, as an alternative to, the Christmas lesson. If you are studying Christmas around the world you can spend a week looking at Jewish traditions. Use some of the suggested books to explain the meaning of Hanukkah.

LETTER/SOUND ASSOCIATIONS: Notice a different way to spell the long a sound in the word "dreidle," even though there is no "a" in the word. Note that the double consonant "kk" in Hanukkah makes only one sound. Introduce the "tw" sound at the beginning of "twirl." List other words that begin with this blend.

RHYMING WORDS: Here is another ABCB pattern poem. The two pairs of rhyming words are spelled with matching letters ("spin"/"begin" and "fast"/"past"). Take note of the placement of rhyming words at the ends of the lines of print.

WORD FAMILIES: Along with some of the more common rhyming families represented in this poem are the following:

"ast" (fast, past, cast, last, mast, vast, etc.)

"oon" (soon, moon, balloon. croon, raccoon, etc.)

From *Daily Poetry* published by GoodYearBooks. Copyright © 1995 Carol Simpson.

VOCABULARY: If you do not have a Jewish child in your class, you might want to locate a Jewish family and have a family member come to your class and explain the dreidle. Perhaps he or she can bring dreidles to share so that students can learn how to play the game and read the symbols on the sides. Ask him or her to explain the lighting of the candles on the menorah and what it means to them.

GRAPHING: After a discussion of Christmas traditions around the world it may be appropriate to graph the celebration that takes place at your students' homes.

AT MY HOUSE WE CELEBRATE					
CHRISTMAS					
HANUKKAH					
OTHER					

If a student signs his or her name beside "OTHER," he or she should explain what happens at his or her house.

COMPARE/CONTRAST: Use a Venn Diagram or similar format to compare and contrast the two major holidays celebrated during December. How are they alike and different?

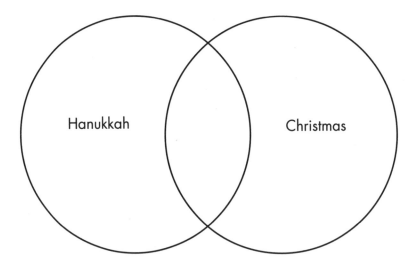

Hanukkah   Christmas

CREATIVE WRITING: There are eight candles on the menorah to represent the eight days of Hanukkah. Children receive a present on each of the days. Have the students write a story about the things they want for each of the eight days of Hanukkah.

From *Daily Poetry* published by GoodYearBooks. Copyright © 1995 Carol Simpson.

Name_____

Here's what I'd like to get for Hanukkah.

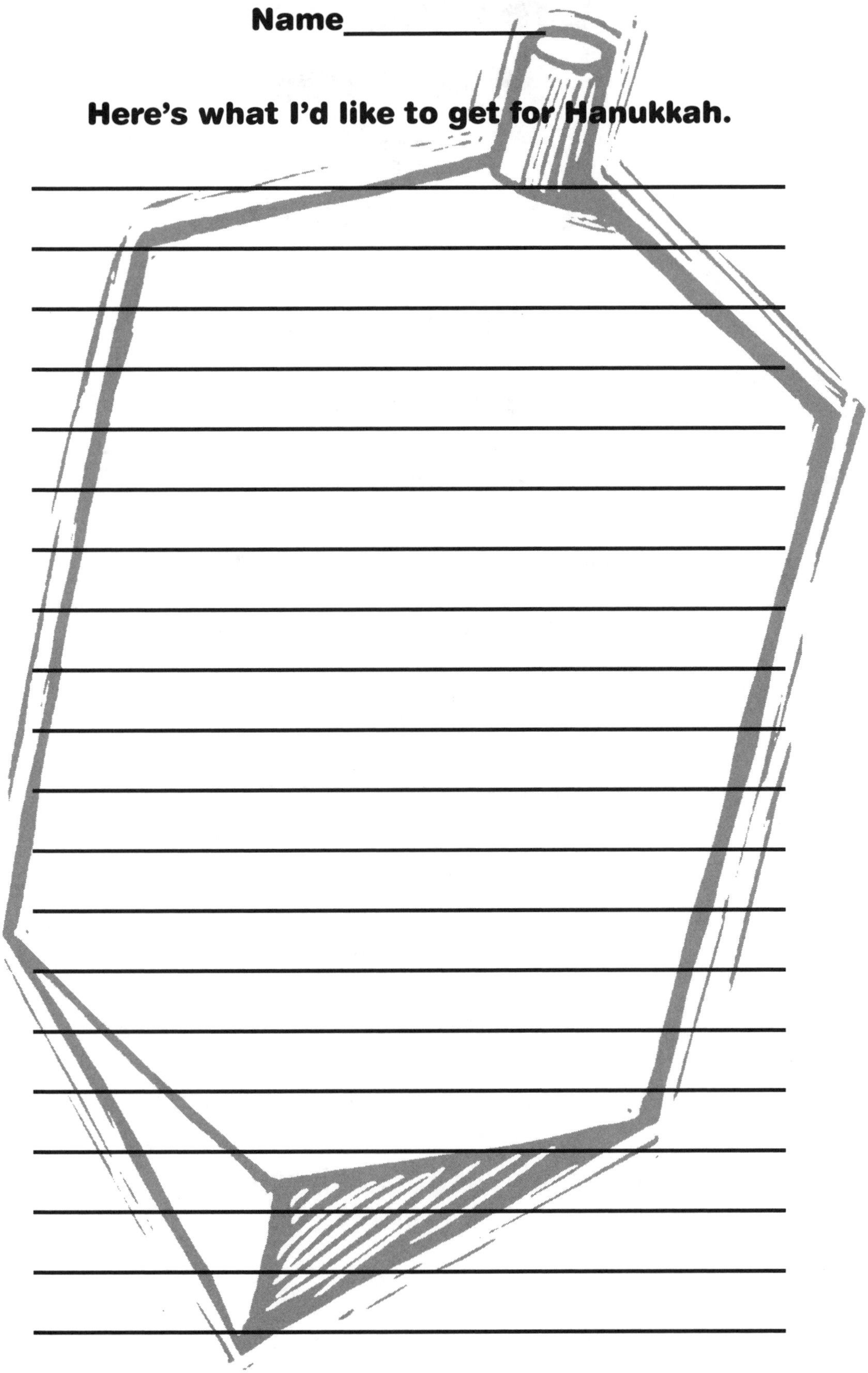

_____

_____

_____

_____

_____

_____

_____

_____

_____

_____

_____

_____

_____

_____

_____

_____

_____

_____

_____

Snowman's Valentine
by
Leland Jacobs

I have a jolly snowman,

The best I've ever had.

I'm giving him a valentine.

That ought to make him glad.

For though he's very handsome

And sound in every part,

I noticed only yesterday

He hasn't any heart.

So quickly with my scissors

And paper red and fine

I've made a fancy little heart;

My snowman's valentine!

From *Daily Poetry* published by GoodYearBooks. Copyright © 1995 Carol Simpson.

OTHER POEMS ABOUT VALENTINE'S DAY:

"If I Were a Valentine" by Kathleen Eiland (1)
"Our Valentine" by Alice DuBois (1)
"The Only One" by Carolyn R. Freeman (1)
"My Valentine" by Clare Miseles (1)
"Valentine!" by Frances Gorman Risser (1)
"Valentine" by Shel Silverstein (3, 15)
"Good Morning" by Traditional English Rhyme (15)
"My Valentine" by Old English Folk Song (15)
"Valentine, Valentine" by Sonja Dunn (17)

BOOKS ABOUT VALENTINE'S DAY:

How Spider Saved Valentine's Day by Robert Kraus
Arthur's Valentine by Marc Brown
Valentine's Day Grump by Rose Greydanus
Freckles and Willie by Margery Cuyler
213 Valentines by Barbara Cohen
Be My Valentine by M. J. Carr
It's Valentine's Day by Jack Prelutsky
Monster Valentines by Joanna Cole
The Mystery of the Missing Red Mitten by Steven Kellogg

From *Daily Poetry* published by GoodYearBooks. Copyright © 1995 Carol Simpson.

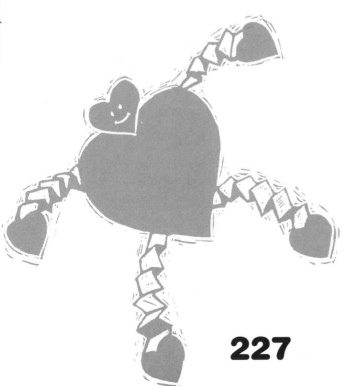

EXTENDING ACTIVITIES

Valentine's Day is a favorite holiday for young children. It is a day when everyone gets and gives something. There is a thrill in reading cards from everyone in your classroom, plus other friends. You will find the traditional "Roses are red . . ." rhyme to rewrite as a creative writing activity.

LETTER/SOUND ASSOCIATIONS: This poem contains both the hard "k" and soft "s" sounds of the letter "c." You can review (or introduce) the soft c sound when the letter is followed by "e," "i," or "y." The "ou" letter combination is found in several words and each one has a slightly different sound for that combination. Find the words "ought," "though," and "sound." The "ou" in ought sounds like "aw." The "ou" in though sounds like long o. The "ou" in sound is the more common one. See if your class can think of other words with the sounds heard in "ought," "though," and "sound."

RHYMING WORDS: Using Unifix® Cubes, see if your students can identify the ABCB pattern of the poem. Rhyming words contain the same spelling patterns except for the slight difference between the words "part"/"heart."

WORD FAMILIES: If you have made a word family spinner, this poem is a good one for spinning and naming a word in a specific family because there are so many families represented. Two of them that you might wish to introduce and expand on charts are:

-ine (valentine, mine, fine, wine, twine, shine, line, etc.)

-ake (make, bake, cake, lake, rake, take, wake, shake, etc.)

From *Daily Poetry* published by GoodYearBooks. Copyright © 1995 Carol Simpson.

VOCABULARY: When writing the poem on a chart, omit the word "jolly" in the first line of the poem. Try temporarily replacing it with other words that can describe a snowman. When a list of possible words is made, write the first letter of the word jolly. If the word is not guessed, write the next letter. You might give the clue that it rhymes with Molly. When students figure out the poet's word, write it on the chart. Find and underline all contractions. Using sticky notes, write the two words for each contraction and see if students can match up the two words to one word. Find the word that uses "'s" not to indicate a contraction but to show ownership.

EXTEND WITH A BOOK: *The Mystery of the Missing Red Mitten* by Steven Kellogg is not one of your traditional Valentine's Day stories. However, it matches the idea of the poem. Share the book and then compare and contrast the two snowmen. How is the book like the poem? How are the two different?

ART PROJECT: You can, of course, make valentine cards at this time of the year. Another project is to make heart people. The head is a small heart, the body is a larger heart, and the arms and legs are strips of paper folded like an accordion with heart shaped hands and feet on the ends. Glue the parts together. Have the children name their heart people. Display them on the bulletin board.

FIELD TRIP/SOCIAL STUDIES: Visit the post office to see how valentines are sent to and received at homes around your town. Talk about the mail carrier as a community helper. Ask students to write an experience story about the field trip when you get back to class.

GRAPHING: Most valentines are either funny or pretty. Make a graph like the one below, and have the students write their names on their favorite kind. Be sure to discuss and measure the results when finished.

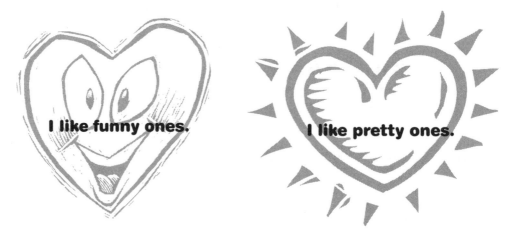

I like funny ones.

I like pretty ones.

CREATIVE WRITING: There are more variations of the traditional "Roses are red . . . ." verse than one can count. Write numerous examples on the board. Get ideas from your students. Give them a basic pattern for trying to write their own verses. Indicate with dark lines the words that need to rhyme.

From *Daily Poetry* published by GoodYearBooks. Copyright © 1995 Carol Simpson.

Roses are red

Violets are green

Your smile is the friendliest

I've ever seen.

Name_____

Roses are red

Violets are_____.

_____

_____

_____

_____

_____

_____

_____

_____

_____

_____

_____

_____

_____

_____?

The Youthful Lincoln
by
Margaret E. Bruner

When Lincoln was a growing boy,

He had few books—not any toy;

He had no lovely shaded light

That he could read beneath at night.

And yet he had the will to learn,

And while the fire logs would burn,

Beside their blaze he often read,

Before he sought his humble bed.

And if perhaps we pause when we

Grow tired, and think of hardships he

Endured, and yet grew kind and strong,

We shall not be discouraged long.

OTHER POEMS ABOUT THE PRESIDENTS:

"On Lincoln's Birthday" by Elaine V. Emans (1)
"Lincoln" by Alice Crowell Hoffman (1)
"As One Lad to Another" by Alice Crowell Hoffman (1)
"You Cannot Tell" by Daisy Jenney Clay (1)
"To Meet Mr. Lincoln" by Eve Mirriam (2, 14, 15)
"Lincoln" by Nancy Byrd Turner (3)

BOOKS ABOUT THE PRESIDENTS:

If You Grew Up with Abraham Lincoln by Ann McGovern
A Picture Book of Abraham Lincoln by David A. Adler
Abraham Lincoln by Kathie Billingslea Smith
Abraham Lincoln by Margaret Davidson
Abraham Lincoln by Ingri and Edgar D'Aulaire
True Stories About Abraham Lincoln by Ruth Belov Gross
If You Grew Up with George Washington by Ruth Belov Gross
A Visit to Washington, D.C. by Jill Krementz
George Washington's Breakfast by Jean Fritz
A Man Named Washington by Gertrude Norman
A Picture Book of George Washington by David A. Adler
A Birthday for General Washington by Johanna Johnston
George and the Cherry Tree by Aliki
The First Book of Presidents by Harold Coy
John F. Kennedy by Andrew Langley
Ronald Reagan: An All American by June Behrens

EXTENDING ACTIVITIES

The poem of the week is about Abraham Lincoln. It is not meant to suggest, however, that you concentrate only on Lincoln or any other particular President for this lesson. Find out how familiar your students are with famous names in our country's history. See which former Presidents they might know, and select a few to study further.

LETTER/SOUND ASSOCIATIONS: Look at the spelling of the word Lincoln. There is a silent letter in that word. Which letter does not make a sound? Identify and examine the silent letters in the words "light"/"night." What other words in this poem have silent letters? Find a word that begins with "h" and rhymes with "mumble." Find a word that begins with "bl" and rhymes with "haze." Think of other riddle rhymes in this poem that you might present.

RHYMING WORDS: Each verse contains two rhyming pairs. Most pairs are spelled in the same way. The second verse contains pairs with different spellings: "learn"/"burn" and "read"/"bed" are not spelled with the same endings. Underline the pairs of rhyming words in the same marker color. Where are all of the rhyming words located?

WORD FAMILIES: Two word families that you might wish to put on charts at this time are:

"ight" (night, light, right, sight, bright, fright, etc.)
"ould" (would, could, should)

Remember to let students help supply the words that you put on a word family chart.

From *Daily Poetry* published by GoodYearBooks. Copyright © 1995 Carol Simpson.

VOCABULARY: There are words in the poem that may need additional explanation to be understood. If you have shared a Lincoln biography, your students will better understand the candle light, the humble bed, and the hardships he endured.

SOCIAL STUDIES: Prepare a time line of the past Presidents. You may not want to list them all—only the ones that your children might recognize. Choose two or three to study further. If your students already know much about Washington and Lincoln, perhaps you would select Presidents John Kennedy, Andrew Jackson, and Teddy Roosevelt for more in-depth study. If your children do not yet have much knowledge about Washington and Lincoln, you will probably want to stick with those familiar names. As you learn more about a former President, compare his life with life today. We have honored some of our past leaders in various ways. From statues to street names, from libraries to coins, how many Presidents' names can you find in or near your home town?

GRAPHING: Select three to five names of Presidents with whom students are most familiar. Ask students what they know or remember about the names selected. Have them graph their favorite President by coloring in a square or writing their names in the appropriate spaces. Talk about the results of the graph.

Washington						
Lincoln						
Reagan						
Bush						
Clinton						

CREATIVE WRITING: Use the following idea for a creative writing activity: Pretend you grew up with one of the Presidents of long ago. Write about your life. You will want to have read or listened to nonfiction books and material about the President you choose. Try to write about the differences between life then and life as we know it today.

Name_____

If I grew up with _____
my life would be different._____

_____

_____

_____

_____

_____

_____

_____

_____

_____

_____

_____

_____

_____

_____

Easter Daisies
by
Aileen Fisher

Scurry, Rabbit,

hurry, Rabbit,

sleek and gray and furry Rabbit,

with your puff of tail.

Find the daisies still in hiding

on the hill where Spring is striding,

tell them without fail:

"Hurry, daisies,

scurry, lazies,

willow cats are purry, daisies,

Winter's really done.

Easter's coming! Every bonnet

should have Easter trimmings on it!"

Tell them, Rabbit.

RUN !

From *Daily Poetry* published by GoodYearBooks. Copyright © 1995 Carol Simpson.

OTHER POEMS ABOUT EASTER:

"One More Time" by Margaret Hillert (1)
"Easter Eggs" by Winifred C. Marshall (1)
"An Easter Puzzle" by Alice DuBois (1)
"The Easter Egg Hunt" by Winifred C. Marshall (1)
"Easter's Coming" by Aileen Fisher (4)
"Listen, Rabbit" by Aileen Fisher (15)

BOOKS ABOUT EASTER:

The Candy Egg Bunny by Lisl Weil
Bunny Trouble by Hans Wilhelm
The *Peter Rabbit* series by Beatrix Potter
Happy Easter, Little Critter by Mercer Mayer
The Easter Egg Farm by Mary Hane Auch
The Big Bunny and the Easter Eggs by Steven Kroll
More Bunny Trouble by Hans Wilhelm
Cranberry Easter by Wende Devlin
We Celebrate Easter by Bobbie Kalman
Silly Tilly and the Easter Bunny by Lillian Hoban
Golden Egg Book by Margaret Brown
Easter Poems by Myra Cohn Livingston

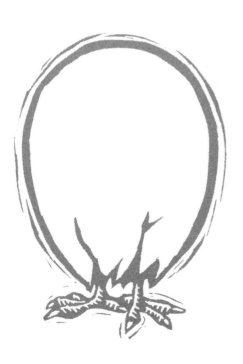

EXTENDING ACTIVITIES

Easter is a holiday that heralds the arrival of spring. We think of bunnies and flowers, of hats and eggs. The bunny in the poem has a job to do: tell the daisies that spring is coming and they should appear again.

LETTER/SOUND ASSOCIATIONS: The poem is filled with rhyming words in the "urry" family. Find all the words in this family and underline them. Say the word that begins with "f" ("furry"). Say the one that begins with "h" ("hurry"). The two "r' s" in these words make only one sound. What other words in the poem have double consonants that make single sounds? There are quite a few! Find them and underline or circle them. Which word starts with w- and rhymes with pillow? Look for blends with the letter "s" ("sl," "st," "sc," "sp"). Find and name the words with "sh," "th," and "wh" in this poem.

RHYMING WORDS: This poem is a bit unusual in that each verse has seven lines instead of an even four or six or eight. Locate the words that rhyme. See if students can identify the AAABCCB pattern of each verse. You may want to use markers and Unifix® Cubes to make a visual picture of the pattern. In the second verse, the -CC- part of the rhyming pattern requires that you say two words in order to rhyme with one word ("bonnet"/"on it"). You will find lots of words that have rhyming sounds besides the intended rhymes at the ends of the lines of print.

From *Daily Poetry* published by GoodYearBooks. Copyright © 1995 Carol Simpson.

WORD FAMILIES: As mentioned previously, there are lots of opportunities to look at rhyming words in this poem of the week. Two word families that you might want to expand onto charts this week are:

"eek" (sleek, week, cheek, peek, creek, etc.)

"ind" (find, kind, mind, wind, grind, bind, etc.)

VOCABULARY: Find words and phrases that describe the rabbit in the poem. Using sticky notes, replace the words "sleek" and "grey" and "furry" with other words that describe rabbits. Point out that the word rabbit begins with a capital letter every time it is found in the poem. Explain that it is meant as a name just like students' names, and is therefore capitalized. Easter is a proper noun. The poet also considers the seasons (Spring, Winter) as proper nouns. What are proper nouns? Bonnet is another word for _____ . Are willow cats "purry"? To what plant is the poet referring?

EXTEND A BOOK: Share the story of *The Candy Egg Bunny* by Lisl Weil. Some of your students believe very strongly in the Easter Bunny. Others will be certain that there is no such thing and will eagerly say so. This story makes doubters rethink their disbelief. Believers will say, "I told you so." Each student in class can contribute a page to a collection of decorated eggs. Cut paper in an egg shape, distribute, let students decorate, and bind into a book. No stories are necessary—just pretty eggs. Students might write their names in the form of a sentence such as:

The candy egg bunny made this egg for _____

Emergent readers will delight in "reading" this book at home if they can read the names of their friends from school.

SCIENCE: Prepare a collection of nonfiction materials on rabbits. Let small groups of students gather information on various kinds of rabbits or hares and share their findings in the form of a written oral report. Rabbits often are hard to see in their natural habitats because they are camouflaged. Discuss the concept of camouflage. What other animals are camouflaged? Are people ever camouflaged?

MATH: Rabbits multiply quickly. Prepare some math multiplication problems dealing with rabbits. If you keep them simple, first- and second-graders will be able to understand them. Make them more difficult for older students who have been exposed to, and perhaps tried to memorize, multiplication tables.

CREATIVE WRITING: Most schools have an annual spring break sometime around Easter. Many families plan a getaway to a warm climate for a few days at this time. Ask your students about their spring break plans. Have them write stories that tell what they plan to do, whether it requires traveling or not.

Name_____

During spring break I plan to

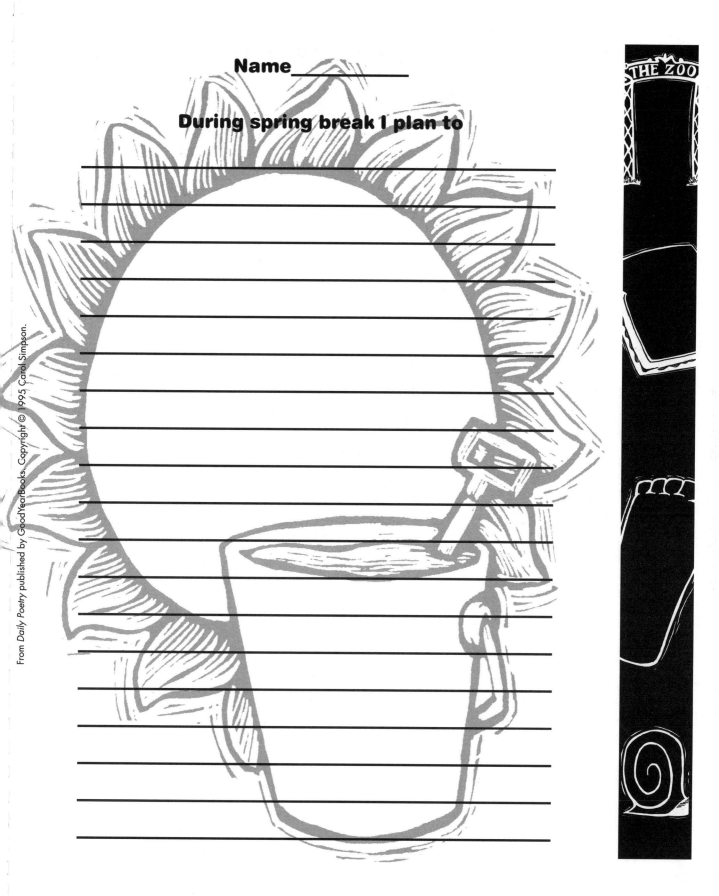

_____

_____

_____

_____

_____

_____

_____

_____

_____

_____

_____

_____

_____

_____

_____

_____

FANTASY

The four poems in this unit are strictly for fun and can be used at any time they fit into your busy schedule. Any time is a good time to "Just Imagine" silly situations. Students of all ages will enjoy the humor in the poem, "Have You Ever Seen?" plus the trade books and other poems suggested. This topic presents many opportunities for students to create their own humorous situations. The middle of the winter might be a good time to look at "Monsters" or "Dinosaurs." By imagining how different life would be if we had to live with either of these potentially dangerous creatures, idle minds might be diverted from thinking about the cold weather outside. The "Sand and Sea" theme might be appropriate near the end of the school year when some students are planning trips to the beach for their summer vacations.

From *Daily Poetry* published by GoodYearBooks. Copyright © 1995 Carol Simpson.

Have You Ever Seen?
Anonymous

Have you ever seen a sheet on a river bed?
Or a single hair from a hammer's head?
Has the foot of a mountain any toes?
And is there a pair of garden hose?

Does the needle ever wink its eye?
Why doesn't the wing of a building fly?
Can you tickle the ribs of a parasol?
Or open the trunk of a tree at all?

Are the teeth of a rake ever going to bite?
Have the hands of a clock any left or right?
Can the garden plot be deep and dark?
And what is the sound of the birch's bark?

OTHER POEMS THAT SPARK YOUR IMAGINATION:

"I Wonder" by Laura Arlon (1)

"Oh Did You Hear?" by Shel Silverstein (2, 14)

"If I Were A . . . " by Karla Kuskin (2, 14)

"If We Walked on Our Hands" by Beatrice Schenk de Regniers (2, 14)

"A Funny Man" by Natalie Joan (2, 14)

"The Folk Who Live in Backward Town" by Mary Ann Hoberman (2, 14)

"The Purple Cow" by Gelett Burgess (3, 13)

"Alligator Pie" by Dennis Lee (3)

"Humpty Dumpty Went to the Moon" by Michael Rosen (7)

"At Sea in the House" by Stanley Cook (7)

"Two Funny Men" by Spike Milligan (7)

"Don't Panic" by Eric Finney (8)

"Have You Ever Thought?" by Jacqueline Brown (8)

"Big Boots" by Irene Rawnsley (10)

"Spaghetti" by Shel Silverstein (21)

"If The World Was Crazy" by Shel Silverstein (21)

"Be Glad Your Nose is On Your Face" by Jack Prelutsky (22)

BOOKS THAT SPARK YOUR IMAGINATION:

That's Good! That's Bad! by Margery Cuyler
Tuesday by David Weisner
Jumanji by Chris Van Allsburg
Imogene's Antlers by David Small
The Big Orange Splot by Daniel Pinkwater
The Boy Who Was Followed Home by Margaret Mahy
Animals Should Definitely Not Act Like People by Judi Barrett
Animals Should Definitely Not Wear Clothing by Judi Barrett

From *Daily Poetry* published by GoodYearBooks. Copyright © 1995 Carol Simpson.

The Red Balloon by Albert Lamorisse
James and the Giant Peach by Roald Dahl
The Dream Book by Margaret Wise Brown
Would You Rather . . . by John Burningham
If You Give a Mouse a Cookie by Laura Numeroff
If You Give a Moose a Muffin by Laura Numeroff
Roger's Umbrella by Daniel Pinkwater
Happy Hippopotami by Bill Martin, Jr.
The *Stupids* series by James Marshall
Two Bad Ants by Chris Van Allsburg
Could Be Worse! by James Stevenson
Weird Parents! by Audrey Wood
King Bidgood's in the Bathtub by Audrey Wood
Fortunately by Remy Charlip
Dogs Don't Eat Sneakers by Laura Numeroff
Once Upon a Time by John Prater
Silly Sally by Audrey Wood

EXTENDING ACTIVITIES

The Fantasy unit is filled with funny poems, stories, and activities that will stir the imaginations of your students. There is a wealth of good literature that will elicit laughter and surprise from your students. Plan, if you can, to read an assortment of the books and poems listed. And encourage your students to try to write some imaginative stories of their own.

LETTER/SOUND ASSOCIATIONS: Most lower case letters of the alphabet, as well as a lot of word families, are represented within the text of this poem. If you are working on finding isolated letters or word families, try using your spinners, as described in "How to Use this Book" (page 1). The controlled "ar," "or," "er," and "ir" are to be found in the poem. You can practice or review the "ee" sound in many words. There are good examples for introducing or reviewing syllabication rules for two-syllable words. Find a word that rhymes with "sing" and begins with "w."

RHYMING WORDS: Underline the rhyming pairs with different colors of markers. With the exception of "dark"/"bark," every pair of rhyming words contains two different spelling patterns. You may find it helpful to list other words that contain these differences. Each verse has an easily recognizable AABB pattern of rhyme. You will notice a lack of any distinctive rhythm to this poem.

From *Daily Poetry* published by GoodYearBooks. Copyright © 1995 Carol Simpson.

WORD FAMILIES: Many word families are included in this poem. For charting purposes, you may want to isolate and list words for the following:

"ink" (wink, sink, mink, think, stink, blink, etc)

"eet" (sheet, meet, greet, feet, sweet, etc)

VOCABULARY: The obvious thing to do with this poem, as soon as it is first introduced, is to discuss the words with more than one meaning. Talk about the humor in this poem. With eyes closed, imagine the scenes that are suggested in the words.

SILLY ART: Ask your students to try illustrating the ridiculous suggestions made in the poem. Mount the pictures around the poetry chart and place it on a bulletin board where everyone can see.

MAKE A CLASS BOOK: The poem suggests many funny scenes. If they put their minds to the task, there are lots of other funny things that students can imagine. Ask everyone to complete the following sentence and illustrate their idea. Bind the pictures into a book with tape or binding rings. Add a cover.

It would be silly if _____ .

Silly Sally by Audrey Wood offers some silly ideas.

WRITE A STORY FOR A WORDLESS PICTURE BOOK: Select a funny wordless picture book, such as *Tuesday* by David Weisner. As students toss out ideas for dialogue between characters in the story, write their ideas on sticky notes cut in the shape of speech bubbles, and place them on the pages of the book. They are fun to read, and they can easily be removed. Your students will enjoy "reading" their story because they have ownership of the words. If your students find it too difficult to write dialogue for speech bubbles, try a telling of the story events on each page by using regular rectangular or square sticky notes mounted on the pages. The children's sense of ownership of the story will make it a favorite for silent reading time.

WORDS WITH MULTIPLE MEANINGS: Select words from the poem, as well as other words with multiple meanings, and discuss those multiple meanings. Ask the students to try illustrating some of them. Some examples of such words are:

BED   1. the bottom of the river 2. a place to sleep
BARK   1. the outside covering of a tree 2. a dog sound
FLY   1. an insect 2. what an airplane does
BAT   1. a flying animal 2. a wooden stick used in baseball 3. to wink— as in "bat an eyelash"
FACE   1. the part of your head that contains eyes, nose, mouth 2. the dial of a clock with twelve numbers 3. to look at someone eye to eye
BEAR   1. a furry mammal 2. to carry 3. to tolerate

CREATIVE WRITING: Brainstorm another list of silly scenes. Ask students to pretend they saw something very strange, something highly unlikely, and write a persuasive story to make it believable.

From *Daily Poetry* published by GoodYearBooks. Copyright © 1995 Carol Simpson.

Name_____

You probably won't believe this, but I saw

What's That?
by
Florence Perry Heide

What's that?

Who's there?

There's a great huge horrible horrible

creeping up the stair!

A huge big terrible terrible

with creepy crawly hair!

There's a ghastly grisly ghastly

with seven slimy eyes!

And flabby grabby tentacles

of a gigantic size!

He's crept into my room now,

he's leaning over me.

I wonder if he's thinking

how delicious I will be.

From *Daily Poetry* published by GoodYearBooks. Copyright © 1995 Carol Simpson.

OTHER POEMS ABOUT MONSTERS:

"Something is There" by Lilian Moore (3)
"Song of the Ogres" by W. H. Auden (3)
"The Bogeyman" by Jack Prelutsky (3)
"The Troll" by Jack Prelutsky (3)
"How to Tell Goblins from Elves" by Monica Shannon (3)
"Gumble" by Michael Dugan (3)
"Slithergadee" by Shel Silverstein (3)
"Ms. Whatchamacallit Thingamajig" by Miriam Chaikin (3)
"The Bogus-Boo" by James Reeves (3)
"The Spangled Pandemonium" by Palmer Brown (3)
"The Creature in the Classroom" by Jack Prelutsky (3)
"Under the Stairs" by Daphne Lister (7)
"We've Got a Wa Wa" by Rony Robinson (7)
"The Sick Young Dragon" by John Foster (7)
"The Small Ghostie" by Barbara Ireson (11)

BOOKS ABOUT MONSTERS:

The Baby UGGS Are Hatching by Jack Prelutsky
Seven Little Monsters by Maurice Sendak
Swamp Monsters by Mary Blount Christian
There's a Monster Eating My House by Art Cumings
The Hungry Thing by Jan Slepian and Ann Seidler
The Very Worst Monster by Pat Hutchins
Rude Giants by Audrey Wood
Where the Wild Things Are by Maurice Sendak
Little Monsters by Jan Pienkowski
One Hungry Monster by Susan O'Keefe
There's a Nightmare in My Closet by Mercer Mayer
There's Something in My Attic by Mercer Mayer
Clyde Monster by Robert Crowe
The After-School Monster by Marissa Moss
Liza Lou and the Yeller Belly Swamp by Mercer Mayer
Little Monster at Home by Mercer Mayer
Beauty and the Beast by Walt Disney
The BFG by Roald Dahl

EXTENDING ACTIVITIES

Here is a just-for-fun lesson that will tickle the imaginations of students at any grade level. Why not read some of the suggested books without showing any pictures and ask your students to draw what they think is described in the story?

LETTER/SOUND ASSOCIATIONS: Locate and label the long and short "i" and long and short "e" words. There are several words with the "cr" blend to underline and name. Look at the hard and soft sounds of the letter "g" within the text of this poem. Many words contain double vowels or consonants. Use these words to examine the fact that two of the same letters usually make a single sound when put together. You will find words that present the "wh" and "th" sounds. Take a look, also, at the "gh" sound at the beginning of "ghastly."

RHYMING WORDS: This 14-line poem has an unusual rhyming pattern. The first six lines appear to fit together in an ABCBDB pattern and the remaining eight lines contain two sets of ABCB patterns. Look at the different spelling patterns of "there"/"stair"/"hair" and "eyes"/"size." After a second reading of the poem, let your students chime in on the rhyming words.

WORD FAMILIES: Two different rhyming patterns that you might use in making word family charts are:

"air" (hair, pair, stair, chair, air, fair, lair, etc.)

"ept" (crept, slept, kept, wept, swept, adept, etc.)

From *Daily Poetry* published by GoodYearBooks. Copyright © 1995 Carol Simpson.

VOCABULARY: Using sticky notes, temporarily replace the word "delicious," in the last line of the poem, with other words that make sense. Introduce the word "tentacles" and explain its meaning. Replace the word with one of clearer meaning if necessary. Underline all of the adjectives in the poem. There are three words in the poem that are used both as an adjective and a noun. What is a terrible terrible or a horrible horrible or a ghastly ghastly? Which word is the adjective and which one is the noun? You may need to explain the words "ghastly" and "grisly" to younger students. Be sure to discuss and explain the use of the question mark, exclamation mark, and period as they are used at the ends of the sentences. There are numerous contraction words to split into two complete words. If you will use sticky notes and place them around the edge of the poetry chart, your students can use free time to match the contractions and sticky notes as a language activity.

DRAW THE MONSTER: Distribute large pieces of drawing paper. Ask students to listen carefully to the words that describe the monster in the poem and then to draw a picture of him. Did they include creepy crawly hair, seven slimy eyes, and flabby grabby tentacles? Encourage the children to draw a big picture rather than one that is too small to include any scary detailing. Allow time for the students to explain their renderings of the scary monsters.

OPPOSITES: Every descriptive phrase makes the monster sound big, bad, and ugly. Using sticky notes, change the negative adjectives to positive ones. How does the appearance of the monster change, in the children's imaginations, when positive adjectives are used?

CREATIVE WRITING: Mercer Mayer's two books, *There's a Nightmare in My Closet and There's Something in My Attic,* should help each student get ideas for a story writing activity about something that lives in their room. When students write their stories, they should try to describe their monster and then tell how they know that it is there.

EXTEND WITH A BOOK: Share Jan Slepian and Ann Seidler's story of *The Hungry Thing*. The story is quite humorous because of the way the silly animal speaks when it talks about food. Brainstorm a list of common foods. Try switching some of the beginning sounds and making up your own list of foods for the hungry creature.

MAKE MASKS: Get creative with paper plates, construction paper of all colors, and some crepe paper streamers. Make monster masks that the children can wear when the poem is shared. Dramatize the monster creeping up the stairs.

GRAPHING: Make a graph that lists four or five monster characteristics, such as sharp claws, sharp teeth, big ears, or a big nose. Students will write their name or color in a space to indicate:

THE SCARIEST THING ABOUT A MONSTER IS ITS:					
SHARP CLAWS					
SHARP TEETH					
BIG EARS					
BIG NOSE					

Name_____

I know there's something living in my room because_____

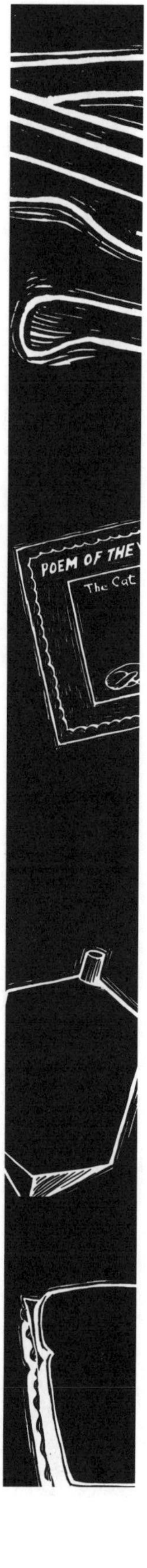

_____

_____

_____

_____

_____

_____

_____

_____

_____

_____

_____

_____

_____

_____

POEM OF THE Y
The Cat

Company
by
Bobbi Katz

I'm fixing a lunch for a dinosaur.

Who knows when one might come by?

I'm pulling up all the weeds I can find.

I'm piling them high as the sky.

I'm fixing a lunch for a dinosaur.

I hope he will stop by soon.

Maybe he'll just walk down my street

And stop for lunch at noon.

OTHER POEMS ABOUT DINOSAURS:

"Pachycephalosaurus" by Richard Armour (2, 14)
"Long Gone" by Jack Prelutsky (3, 6)
"Brontosaurus" by Gail Kredenser (3)
"So Big" by Max Fatchen (7)
"Sauruses" by Sonja Dunn (18)
"Always Be Polite When You Boss an Allosaurus" by Brod
Bagert (20)
"The Dinosaur Difference" by Brod Bagert (20)
"Mini Monsters" by Brod Bagert (20)
"Poor Dinosaur Children" by Brod Bagert (20)
"If I Had a Brontosaurus" by Shel Silverstein (21)

BOOKS ABOUT DINOSAURS:

Tyrannosaurus Was a Beast by Jack Prelutsky
Dinosaurs (First Discovery Series) by Gallimard Jeunesse
and others
Dinosaurs (Eye Openers Series) by Angela Royston
First Facts About Prehistoric Animals by Gina Phillips
King of the Dinosaurs by Michael Berenstain
The Incredible Dinosaurs by Rita Golden Gelman
The Dinosaur Alphabet Book by Jerry Pallotta
Little Grunt and the Big Egg by Tomie dePaola
Danny and the Dinosaur by Syd Hoff
If the Dinosaurs Came Back by Bernard Most
Whatever Happened to the Dinosaurs? by Bernard Most
Home for a Dinosaur by Eileen Curran
There's a Dinosaur in the Park by Rodney Martin
The Enormous Egg by Oliver Butterworth
David Dreaming of Dinosaurs by Keith Faulkner
The Littlest Dinosaurs by Bernard Most
Dinosaur Encore by Patricia Mullins
Dinosaurs, Dinosaurs by Byron Barton
Dinosaur Chase by Carolyn Otto
The Dinosaur Who Lived in My Backyard by
B. G. Hennessy
Dinosaurs by Gail Gibbons

EXTENDING ACTIVITIES

Children love dinosaurs. Nothing seems to stimulate their curiosity more than the study, fanciful or scientific, of these giants of the past. Whether you are taking a close look at specific animals or imagining how things might be if dinosaurs were with us today, children will thoroughly enjoy this lesson.

LETTER/SOUND ASSOCIATIONS: All letters of the alphabet except q, v, and z can be found and circled, if letter recognition is still necessary for your group. You might ask for a word that begins like "dog" or use another appropriate beginning sound. Find a word that ends like "hop," or other appropriate ending sound. Find a word that starts with "w" and rhymes with "seeds." The two sounds of "ow" can be examined in the words "knows" and "down." List other words with the same sound and spelling pattern. There are words in the poem with spelling patterns that include seemingly silent letters: "knows," "might," "high," and "walk." Can your students name other words with the same spelling patterns? Find and circle each letter "o" and examine the many sounds of that letter besides the long and short sounds.

RHYMING WORDS: There are two pairs of rhyming words in this ABCBDEFE poem. You can use your Unifix® Cubes to discover this pattern. Be sure to underline or circle your rhyming words in different colors. After a second reading of the poem, let your children chime in on the rhyming words. Be sure to ask which two words sound the same.

From *Daily Poetry* published by GoodYearBooks. Copyright © 1995 Carol Simpson.

WORD FAMILIES: Two unusual spelling patterns to consider for charting are:

"unch" (lunch, bunch, munch, hunch, crunch, brunch, etc.)
"alk" (walk, talk, chalk, stalk, etc.)

VOCABULARY: When you first share the poem, use sticky notes or thick paper to hide the word "lunch" in the first, fifth, and last lines. See if your students can predict an appropriate word to fit those places. What words in the rest of the poem provide clues to the missing word? Take a look at the words with the "-ing" suffix. Compare the root word "pile" to the word "piling" and discover what happened to the silent "e." Look at other words with the same suffix, comparing them to the root words, and see if your students can discover any spelling rules. Find the compound word and the contractions and separate them into two words. Look at the punctuation marks at the ends of the lines. What is the questioning word in the second line?

MATH: The dinosaurs lived millions of years ago. How much is a million? Try to collect one thousand of something, such as straws or toothpicks or Cheerios®. Compare one thousand to one million. How many thousands are needed to make one million? Be sure to make your counting easier by first bundling tens, then hundreds, and finally one thousand. Can you count higher? The number you determine to be your stopping point will depend upon the level of your group. If you work with 5- to 6-year olds you may want to stop at 100.

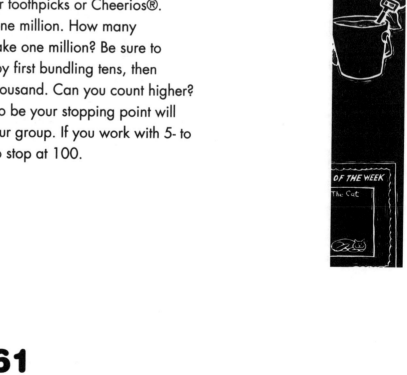

GRAPHING: Children seem to know at least four or five of the more common dinosaurs we study. Ask them to select their favorite one. The choices you give your group will depend upon the kinds of dinosaurs they know at the time. Here are some familiar names you might use.

MY FAVORITE DINOSAUR IS:					
TYRANNOSAURUS REX					
STEGOSAURUS					
BRONTOSAURUS					
TRICERATOPS					

SCIENCE PROJECTS: Brainstorm a list of six to eight dinosaurs that your students think they might like to study further. Allow them to sign up to work in a small group to read about and share their findings on a particular dinosaur. Ask them to make a mural of their dinosaur's habitat. They will want to look in nonfiction sources to find out when their dinosaur lived, whether it ate meat or plants, how big it was, and anything special about their animal. Here is an excellent opportunity to use your measuring "feet" (pieces of construction paper or heavier paper, cut in the shape of the sole of a shoe, and measuring 12" in length) to visualize the actual size of the dinosaurs. You will need a large number of measuring feet in order to accommodate both length and height of some of the ancient creatures. Do you have a room large enough where groups can demonstrate the size of their animal using the measuring feet? Allow the study groups to present their findings as a culminating event.

From *Daily Poetry* published by GoodYearBooks. Copyright © 1995 Carol Simpson.

SORT LITERATURE: Gather a large collection of dinosaur books. Ask your group of emergent readers to sort the books into two piles: the books that are true (nonfiction) and the books that are pretend (fiction). What do the children look for when determining which pile is appropriate? Introduce the words "fiction" and "nonfiction," if your group is ready for that.

EXTEND WITH A BOOK: Bernard Most has written some delightful books about the dinosaurs. Students from kindergarten to third-grade, and beyond, enjoy the humorous look at what would happen *"If the Dinosaurs Came Back,"* or the outrageous explanations for *"Whatever Happened to the Dinosaurs?"* Both of these books can lead to group or whole class collections of additional fanciful ideas on the subjects.

CREATIVE WRITING: Many of the fiction books about dinosaurs ask us to imagine having a dinosaur in our backyard to be our pet or best friend. Ask students to pretend that they were followed home by a dinosaur. How would they take care of it? Do they think their parents would let them keep it? Where would it stay? Would they tell anyone about their new friend? Have them write a story that tells what might happen.

Name _____

A dinosaur followed me home so I _____

_____

_____

_____

_____

_____

_____

_____

_____

_____

_____

_____

_____

_____

_____

The Barracuda
by
John Gardner

Slowly, slowly he cruises,
And slowly, slowly he chooses
Which kind of fish he prefers to take this morning;

Then without warning
The Barracuda opens his jaws, teeth flashing,
And with a horrible, horrible grinding and gnashing,
Devours a hundred poor creatures and feels no remorse.

It's no wonder of course,
That he really ought, perhaps, to change his ways.
"But" (as he says With an evil grin)
"It's actually not my fault, you see!
I've nothing to do with the tragedy;
I open my mouth for a yawn and—ah me—

They all
swim
in!"

"The Barracuda" from *A Child's Bestiary* by John Gardner.
Copyright © 1977 by John Gardner. Reprinted by permission of
Georges Borchardt, Inc. on behalf of the estate of John Gardner.

OTHER POEMS WITH A BEACH AND/OR SEA THEME:

"Sitting In the Sand" by Karla Kuskin (1, 5)
"Sleepy Oyster" by Frances Gorman Risser (1)
"Until I Saw The Sea" by Lilian Moore (2, 3)
"Sea Shell" by Amy Lowell (3)
"The Sea" by Anonymous (3)
"The Shark" by Lord Alfred Douglas (3)
"The Picnic" by Dorothy Aldis (4)
"Seaweed" by Myra Cohn Livingston (4)
"Undersea" by Marchette Chute (5)
"The Fish With the Deep Sea Smile" by Margaret Wise Brown (5)
"The Octopus" by Ogden Nash (6)
"Narwhal" by X. J. Kennedy (6)
"Electric Eel" by X. J. Kennedy (6)
"The Sea" by John Kitching (7)
"The Dolphin" by Alan Bold (7)
"The Sand Castle" by James Kirkup (8)
"At the Sea-Side" by Robert Louis Stevenson (9)

BOOKS ABOUT SAND AND SEA:

A Picture Book of Underwater Life by Theresa Grace
Amazing Fish (Eyewitness Juniors) by Mary Ling
Sharks (Explorer Books) by Della Rowland
First Facts About Giant Sea Creatures by Gina Phillips
The Magic School Bus on the Ocean Floor by Joanna Cole
The Ocean Alphabet Book by Jerry Pallotta
Baby Beluga by Raffi
Plenty of Fish by Millicent Selsam
Swimmy by Leo Lionni
Big Al by Andrew Clements
Sign of the Seahorse by Graeme Base
Fish Faces by Norbert Wu

From *Daily Poetry* published by GoodYearBooks. Copyright © 1995 Carol Simpson.

267

EXTENDING ACTIVITIES

The sand and sea lesson can be a colorful one if you will try the mural art activity. Another good hands-on activity would involve getting a wash tub full of beach sand from say, Florida's west coast if possible, in which there are millions of crushed shells to be discovered under closer examination with a magnifying glass. Children will also delight in discovering the small shells that you can deliberately hide in regular sand. You can select any time of year to do this unit. Try it right before summer vacation or in February to cure the winter blahs.

LETTER/SOUND ASSOCIATIONS: All letters except "q," "x," and "z" can be found and circled, if you need letter identification. There are three spellings of the "au" sound as found in "jaws" and "fault" and "ought." Discover the same "ou" as in the word "ought" in other words with different sounds, such as "devours" and "course." Look at the silent "g" in "gnashing." You can work on the "sh," "ch," "wh," and "th" sounds in this poem. Find a word that rhymes with make and begins with "t." Find a word that ends like "both." Find a word that starts like "flower." You will be able to locate the long and short sounds of all five vowels within the words of this poem. The controlled sounds of "ar," "er," and "or" can be heard and marked.

RHYMING WORDS: The first ten lines of the poem contain adjoining rhyming words at the ends of the lines. The ways/says rhyme is more difficult to determine. You may want to say that they are not actually rhyming words or else call it an off-rhyme. The others have very clear rhyming sounds, some with different spelling patterns. The remaining lines of the poem contain a different rhyming pattern from the AABBCCDDEE of the first ten lines. If you work with older students, you may ask them to try to determine the remaining pattern.

From *Daily Poetry* published by GoodYearBooks. Copyright © 1995 Carol Simpson.

WORD FAMILIES: Two word families that you may choose to put on charts at this time are:

"ought" (ought, bought, fought, brought, thought, etc.)
"awn" (yawn, lawn, dawn, drawn, prawn, fawn, etc.)

VOCABULARY: This poem may be too difficult for very young children to read and understand. You may want to select something easier. If you elect to use "The Barracuda" you will want to introduce and discuss a lot of the unusual words used to describe the big fish. You may need to explain "gnashing," "remorse," "cruises," "devours," and "tragedy." Once children understand the meanings of all of the words, they will be able to picture in their minds the barracuda's swimming along looking for something to eat, and suddenly eating hundreds of little fish in just one gulp.

EXTEND WITH A BOOK: Read *Swimmy* by Leo Lionni. This is a very colorful book about a little black fish whose brothers and sisters (all red) were eaten by a giant tuna one day. Swimmy discovers a school of little red fish just like his family and teaches them a neat trick to help them survive. Cut some sponges in the shape of simple little fish. Provide paint in two colors: red and black. On large drawing or painting paper enough for each student, draw a large fish outline. Let each student illustrate the last scene in the book by sponge painting a lot of red fish swimming in one direction inside the big shape, and then one black fish to be the eye. Cut out the large fish outlines and mount all of them together on a very large blue background. You may want to cut a rippled top line on your blue background to resemble the water's waves.

SCIENCE/ART: Brainstorm a list of all kinds of creatures from the sea. Allow students to sign up in small groups to investigate further one of the choices. Groups will need a selection of nonfiction books and materials for doing their research about sea creatures. Groups can present their findings in the form of a page for a class book. Each page should contain at least one paragraph with facts, plus a picture (drawing or magazine picture) of their animal as it lives in the sea. A culminating activity might be to paint or draw and cut out sea creatures of all kinds for a large mural. Find a wall space where you can mount a very large piece of blue paper (4' x 10' for example) for your background. You may want to cut a rippled top on your blue paper to represent the wavy water. This mural can be very colorful as well as educational for those who make and view it.

MAKE A BOOKLET: Make a simple under the sea booklet for each child by stapling several sheets of paper, writing paper or plain newsprint, to a construction paper back. Cut the sheets of paper in a wavy design at the top, as shown below. Students can write their own stories about water experiences and share them.

From *Daily Poetry* published by GoodYearBooks. Copyright © 1995 Carol Simpson.

GRAPHING: Have your class graph their favorite sea creatures. The four or more choices will depend upon which ones your class knows best. Here is a sample graph of favorite sea creatures.

WHALE					
SHARK					
BARRACUDA					
OCTOPUS					
EEL					
DOLPHIN					

EXPLORE BEACH SAND: Try to get a wash tub full of beach sand for exploration. If possible, get some sand from the west coast of Florida because it is filled with millions of tiny sea shell pieces. Students delight in looking closely at the grains of sand and tiny shell pieces with a magnifying glass or microscope. Many students have collections of sea shells that they will be eager to bring to school to show. If you can get an appropriate book, your students can try to identify their shells by name. Bury some tiny shells in the tub of sand and watch your youngsters delight in finding buried treasure! If you are a traveller, try to collect sand from a variety of beaches for comparison. Keep the sand samples in separate containers (plastic zip type baggies are good) and make sure you label it.

CREATIVE WRITING: Try to locate information about recent findings from sunken ships. Gold coins, jewels, and other treasures are often discovered among the wreckage. Plan a pretend dive with your class. You might even want to name your own sunken ship and locate it on a world map. If you have a scuba diver friend, ask him or her to come in and talk about his or her equipment. When you have done sufficient preparation, ask your students to write about a treasure hunt to the bottom of the sea.

Name _____

I took a trip to the bottom of the sea and I found treasure!

COLORS
AND NUMBERS

Depending upon the level of your students, you may choose not to use the very simple themes of "Colors" and "Numbers." You will find them very helpful, however, if you work with emergent readers because these themes can be used to teach color and number words. You may choose to deal with the color words very early in the year, perhaps the first week, and then follow with number words after the unit about "My World."

Even though the poem for colors is not easy to learn, it is filled with color words, words that your emergent readers need to learn as soon as they are ready.

What Is Pink?
by
Christina Rossetti

What is pink? a rose is pink

By the fountain's brink.

What is red? a poppy's red

In its barley bed.

What is blue? the sky is blue

Where the clouds float thro'.

What is white? a swan is white

Sailing in the light.

What is yellow? pears are yellow,

Rich and ripe and mellow.

What is green? the grass is green,

With small flowers between.

What is violet? clouds are violet

In the summer twilight.

What is orange? why, an orange,

Just an orange!

From *Daily Poetry* published by GoodYearBooks. Copyright © 1995 Carol Simpson.

OTHER POEMS ABOUT COLOR:

"The Painting Lesson" by Frances Greenwood (1)
"Colors and Colors" by Vivian Gouled (1)
"I'm Glad the Sky Is Painted Blue" by Anonymous (3)
"Rhinos Purple, Hippos Green" by Michael Patrick Hearn (3)
"What is Red?" by Mary O'Neill (3)
"Yellow" by David McCord (3)
"The Paint Box" by E. V. Rieu (3)

BOOKS ABOUT COLOR:

Planting a Rainbow by Lois Ehlert
Colors (First Discovery Series) by Gallimard Jeunesse
and others
Winnie the Witch by Korky Paul and Valerie Thomas
Brown Bear, Brown Bear, What Do You See? by Bill Martin, Jr.
The Big Orange Splot by Daniel Pinkwater
Mouse Paint by Ellen Walsh
Bear's Colors by Harriet Ziefert
The Mystery of the Stolen Blue Paint by Steven Kellogg
Lunch by Denise Fleming
The Art Lesson by Tomie dePaola
Little Blue and Little Yellow by Leo Lionni
The Great Blueness by Arnold Lobel

EXTENDING ACTIVITIES

The level of the extending activities you select will depend upon the time of year you choose to present this lesson. If you teach first-grade students, you may want to do color words very early in the year. The poem is difficult to read and understand, but it is useful because of the number of color words the children can try to locate. Avoid the word family charting and instead do the art projects and share many of the other poems and trade books that are listed. If you teach second- or third-grade students, you may want to present this unit at some other time of the year. The poem will be easier for your older students to read and understand because their language arts skills will be more developed.

LETTER/SOUND ASSOCIATIONS: Most letters of the alphabet are included in the words of this poem. They can be found and circled, in alphabetical order, if necessary. The only letters you will not find are "q," "x," and "z." All short and long vowel sounds are present. You might want to locate all of the "a"'s and decide what sound each makes; there are many and they vary. You can work on the double consonant spelling ("ll," "mm," "pp," "ss") as it represents a single sound. Many words have the "wh" sound. There are many blends with "s" ("st," "sk," "sw," "sm') that can be studied by listing other words with the same blends.

Look at the words "by," "sky," and "why." They do not contain a vowel. Which letter represents the vowel sound, and what sound does it make? Compare that sound to the letter "y" in "poppy," "barley," or "yellow." Compare the sound of the letter "g" in "orange" and "green." One is hard, one is soft. Which is which?

From *Daily Poetry* published by GoodYearBooks. Copyright © 1995 Carol Simpson.

RHYMING WORDS: After the first two or three readings of the poem, older children can chime in on the rhyming words. Even though first-graders should understand rhyme, they will probably not understand the second word in many of the rhyming pairs. Look at the spelling differences in "blue"/"thro'," "white"/"light," and "violet"/"twilight."

WORD FAMILIES: First-graders who are learning the color words near the beginning of the year will not be ready to do word families. It is suggested that you wait several weeks before beginning this concept. Second- and third-graders will be ready to do the two families suggested for charting.

"ipe" (ripe, wipe, pipe, swipe, etc.)
"een" (green, between, seen, keen, etc)

VOCABULARY: Color words can be located and underlined or circled, preferably with a marker of the same color. Young children may not understand the color "violet" and may need help in choosing a purple marker when circling or underlining the word. You probably will need to explain and discuss the following words and phrases:

"fountain's brink" "barley bed"
"mellow" "twilight"

Locate the nouns—the things that are listed after each specific color. You may choose to circle them in the color with which they are associated. Some of the nouns are singular and some are plural. What word does the poet mean by "thro'" at the end of the sixth line?

GRAPHING: Distribute small, 2" x 2" pieces of paper and have students color their piece in their favorite color. Your graph should contain all of the eight basic colors, plus pink. Students will glue their color onto the appropriate box on the graph. For first-graders, this may be an introduction to graphing. Be sure to measure and discuss the results of your graph when finished.

RED	**BLUE**	**YELLOW**	**PURPLE**	**ORANGE**	**GREEN**	**BLACK**	**BROWN**	**PINK**

COLOR WORD CHARTS: Ask students to find pictures of animals and foods and other things that feature a particular color. Write the color words on large pieces of oak tag or manila paper. Let students glue their pictures onto the appropriate color word chart.

EXTEND WITH A BOOK: Share the story of *The Big Orange Splot* by Daniel Pinkwater. This is a fanciful story about a man who does not want his house to look just like everyone else's house on his street. The neighbors dislike the strange appearance of his house, until they have spent an evening talking with him about their dreams. Children delight in the illustrations. When the story is finished, let students draw pictures of the house of their dreams. Ask older students to write a paragraph about it.

From *Daily Poetry* published by GoodYearBooks. Copyright © 1995 Carol Simpson.

WRITE A CLASS STORY: Bill Martin, Jr.'s story *Brown Bear, Brown Bear, What Do You See?* is a favorite among primary teachers because it contains color words and simple, predictable text. With your help, the class can make their own version of this book. Each student needs to complete the following sentence by inserting first a color word and then an animal name.

"I see a _____ _____ looking at me."

Examples of words to insert might be "purple parrot" or "green mouse." When all student pages are complete, you need to write the connecting text on the back of those pages. For example:

Student writes: "I see a pink poodle looking at me."
You write: "Pink poodle, pink poodle, what do you see?
Next student writes: "I see a green mouse looking at me."

The title of the class book might be "Students, Students, What Do You See?"

CREATIVE WRITING/SCIENCE: Make rose-colored glasses (or any other color students choose) by putting laminating film, colored with water base marker, in between the frames of construction paper or manila paper glasses.

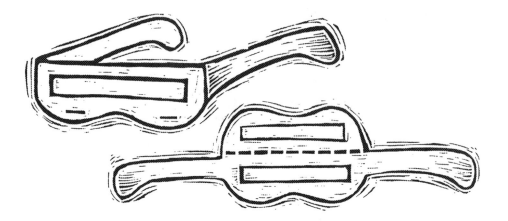

Let the children spend time looking at the world through their colored glasses. Then ask them to write a story about what they see. Is the world prettier? Is it a happier place? Would they like to change the world to that color? Students in first-grade may enjoy drawing a picture of the world around them in its new color rather than trying to write or dictate a story about it.

WRITE A COLOR WORD POEM: The color words offer numerous opportunities for making rhyming phrases. For example:

Red, red . . . jumped in bed
Yellow, yellow . . . a jolly fellow
Brown, brown . . . a funny clown

From *Daily Poetry* published by GoodYearBooks. Copyright © 1995 Carol Simpson.

Children can write their own rhyming pairs. The teacher needs to provide some examples so that students understand the challenge. Here is a way to put the poem on a chart and make the phrases completely interchangeable.

Write only the color words along the left-hand side of the chart paper. On the right-hand side, and adjacent to the color words, cut tiny slits in which to place paper clips in such a way that one side of the clip is on the front side of the chart and the other half of the clip is taped to the back of the chart. The rhyming phrases can be written on oaktag strips and then slipped under the paper clips as children find the appropriate rhyming color words. This kind of interchangeable poetry chart might also be useful for number words and other rhyming situations.

Colors

Red, red

Yellow, yellow

Brown, brown

Green, green

Black, black

Orange, orange

Blue, blue

Purple, purple

Pink, pink,

Colors

Red, red   jumped in bed

Yellow, yellow   a jolly fellow

Brown, brown

Green, green

Black, black

Orange, orange

Blue, blue

Purple, purple

Pink, pink,

I painted my world in a new color.

One, Two, Bubblegum Chew
by
Meguido Zola

One, two,

Bubblegum chew,

Three, four,

Candy store,

Five, six,

Peppermint stick,

Seven, eight,

Sticky date,

Nine, ten,

Start again.

OTHER POEMS ABOUT NUMBERS:

"A Pig Tale" by James Reeves (2, 14)
"Five Little Squirrels" by Anonymous (2, 14)
"Arithmetic" by Carl Sandburg (2, 3, 14)
"Counting" by Lee Bennett Hopkins (4)
"Five Little Monsters" by Eve Mirriam (4)
"Five Little Chickens" by Anonymous (4)
"Seven Little Rabbits" by John Becker (4)
"Old Noah's Ark" Folk Rhyme (4)
"One two . . . three four" by Sonja Dunn (17)

BOOKS ABOUT NUMBERS:

Ten Little Goblins by Avelyn Davidson
Fish Eyes, a Book You Can Count On by Lois Ehlert
Count-a-Saurus by Nancy Blumenthal
The Right Number of Elephants by Jeff Sheppard
What Comes in 2s, 3s, and 4s? by Suzanne Aker
The Twelve Circus Rings by Seymour Chwast
10 for Dinner by Jo Ellen Bogart
26 Letters and 99 Cents by Tana Hoban
One Gorilla by Atsuko Morozumi
Only One by Marc Harshman
Each Orange Had 8 Slices by Paul Giganti, Jr.
Rooster's Off to See the World by Eric Carle
Bunches and Bunches of Bunnies by Louise Matthews
The Doorbell Rang by Pat Hutchins
Bear's Numbers by Harriet Ziefert
Anno's Counting Book by Mitsumasa Anno
Inch by Inch by Leo Lionni
One Bear All Alone by Caroline Bucknall
Ten in a Bed by Allan Ahlberg
12 Ways to Get to 11 by Eve Mirriam
One Hundred Hungry Ants by Elinor J. Pinczes
Count! by Denise Fleming

EXTENDING ACTIVITIES

The main point of this lesson is to review number words. Your first-graders will need to do this rather early in the year. Second- and third-graders may not need number word review, but they might enjoy writing some of their own number poems. Try to locate some of the poems that parody "One, Two, Buckle My Shoe" or write some of your own examples. Look in "How to Use This Book" (page 1) for an example about "possum stew."

LETTER/SOUND ASSOCIATIONS: All lower-case letters of the alphabet can be found and circled except for "j," "q," and "z." The capital "Z" is found in the poet's name. Find a word that rhymes with "late" and starts with "d." Find a word that begins like "child." Find a word that ends like "box." You can do other "Find a word . . . ." hunts that depend upon the level of your group. What vowel sound does the letter "y" make at the end of the words "sticky" and "candy"?

RHYMING WORDS: The rhyming pattern will be easy even for first-graders to find and demonstrate with Unifix® Cubes. After the second or third reading, let your youngsters chime in on the second rhyming word in a pair. Look at the differences in the spelling patterns of the rhyming pairs ("two"/"chew," "four"/"store," "six"/"stick," "eight"/"date," and "ten"/"again").

WORD FAMILIES: Two word families you may want to put on charts at this time are:

"ive" (five, dive, hive, chive, alive, etc.)

"int" (peppermint, hint, mint, glint, tint, etc.)

VOCABULARY: The text of this poem is simple. There will probably be no need to explain any of the words in context. You can change "candy store" to any other kind of store using sticky notes to cover up the original word. The word "sticky" could also be changed to another adjective.

EXTEND WITH A BOOK: Pat Hutchins' book *The Doorbell Rang* is an excellent story to share and then use to demonstrate the math concept of division. Make a plate of paper cookies to distribute, collect, and redistribute each time the doorbell rings. Students can predict how many cookies each child will receive.

WRITE A NUMBER WORD POEM: Take the pattern of the poem of the week, as well as any other parodies of "One, Two, Buckle My Shoe" as a model, and have each student write his or her own poem. Begin by brainstorming lists of words that will rhyme with "two," "four," "six," "eight," and "ten." Can your students write a poem that is based upon a single theme or idea? An example might be a zoo poem that begins:

> 1, 2 busy zoo
> 3, 4 lions roar

and continues with the names of other zoo animals. Look in the introductory section for a food poem with the same pattern.

WORK WITH NUMBER WORDS: On sticky notes make flash cards of the numerals 1-10 and place them around the poetry chart. Students can match them to the number words as a free time activity. Put the lines of the poem on oak tag strips and let students try to arrange the lines in proper sequence in a pocket chart.

Name_____

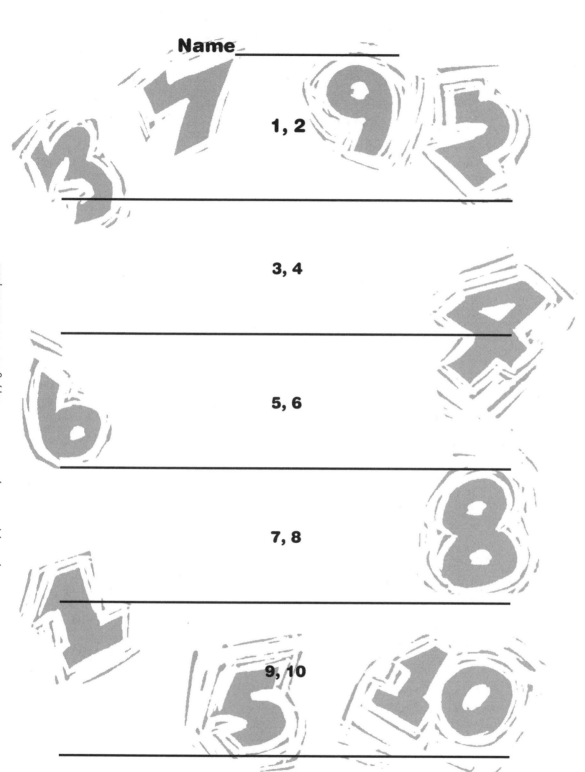

1, 2

3, 4

5, 6

7, 8

9, 10

AUTHOR'S VITA

Carol Simpson has been a first- and second-grade classroom teacher with the District #205 Public Schools in Galesburg, Illinois since the fall of 1971. She joined the whole language movement in 1988 after observing firsthand the exciting things that were happening in primary classrooms of Australia. Carol's husband and son have been very supportive of her extensive travels in pursuit of new educational ideas. Carol has written a book called *Daily Journals,* which was published by GoodYearBooks in the spring of 1993.

NOTES:

NOTES:

NOTES:

NOTES:

NOTES:

NOTES:

NOTES:

NOTES:

NOTES:

NOTES: